Cambridge School
Shakespeare

A Midsummer Night's Dream

Edited by Linda Buckle

Series Editor: Rex Gibson
Director, Shakespeare and Schools Project

CAMBRIDGE
UNIVERSITY PRESS

CAMBRIDGE UNIVERSITY PRESS
Cambridge, New York, Melbourne, Madrid, Cape Town, Singapore, São Paulo

Cambridge University Press
The Edinburgh Building, Cambridge CB2 8RU, UK

www.cambridge.org
Information on this title: www.cambridge.org/9780521618717

First published 1992
Second edition 2000
Third edition 2005
Reprinted 2006, 2007

Printed in the United Kingdom at the University Press, Cambridge

A catalogue record for this publication is available from the British Library

ISBN 978-0-521-61871-7 paperback

ACKNOWLEDGEMENTS
Thanks are due to the following for permission to reproduce illustrations:
Cover, v, vi, vii, viii, ix, x, xi*t*, xii, 6, 44, 46, 68, 102, 155, 157, 167, 168, 169, 170,
171, Donald Cooper/Photostage; xi*b*, 152, 153, 156, 20th Century Fox/The Kobal
Collection/Tursi, Mario; 4, 36, 64, 80, 130, Malcolm Davies Collection © Shakespeare
Birthplace Trust; 22, 76, 100, 140, Robert Barber; 24, Zoë Dominic; 30, 88, The New
Shakespeare Company/John Timbers; 42, Royal Exchange Theatre, Manchester/John
Peters; 54, 132, BBC Photo Library; 56. The Thos. F. and Mig Holte Collection
© Shakespeare Birthplace Trust; 62, Neil Libbert; 66, David Farrell; 74, by per-
mission of the Shakespeare Birthplace Trust; 92, 120, Alastair Muir; 98, © Munch
Museum/Munch–Ellingsen Group, BONO, Oslo, DACS, London 2004; 114, 148, Hull
Truck Theatre Company/Steve Morgan; 166, Edwin Landseer, English 1802–73, *Scene
from A Midsummer Night's Dream. Titania and Bottom*, 1848–61, oil on canvas, 82.0 ×
133.0 cm, Felton Bequest, 1932, National Gallery of Victoria, Melbourne, Australia.

Cover design by Smith

Contents

Cambridge School
Shakespeare

This edition of *A Midsummer Night's Dream* is part of the **Cambridge School Shakespeare** series. Like every other play in the series, it has been specially prepared to help all students in schools and colleges.

This *A Midsummer Night's Dream* aims to be different from other editions of the play. It invites you to bring the play to life in your classroom, hall or drama studio through enjoyable activities that will increase your understanding. Actors have created their different interpretations of the play over the centuries. Similarly, you are encouraged to make up your own mind about *A Midsummer Night's Dream*, rather than having someone else's interpretation handed down to you.

Cambridge School Shakespeare does not offer you a cut-down or simplified version of the play. This is Shakespeare's language, filled with imaginative possibilities. You will find on every left-hand page: a summary of the action, an explanation of unfamiliar words, and a choice of activities on Shakespeare's language, characters and stories.

Between the acts and in the pages at the end of the play, you will find notes, illustrations and activities. These will help to increase your understanding of the whole play.

There are a large number of activities to give you the widest choice to suit your own particular needs. Please don't think you have to do every one. Choose the activities that will help you most.

This edition will be of value to you whether you are studying for an examination, reading for pleasure, or thinking of putting on the play to entertain others. You can work on the activities on your own or in groups. Many of the activities suggest a particular group size, but don't be afraid to make up larger or smaller groups to suit your own purposes.

Although you are invited to treat *A Midsummer Night's Dream* as a play, you don't need special dramatic or theatrical skills to do the activities. By choosing your activities, and by exploring and experimenting, you can make your own interpretations of Shakespeare's language, characters and stories. Whatever you do, remember that Shakespeare wrote his plays to be acted, watched and enjoyed.

Rex Gibson

This edition of *A Midsummer Night's Dream* uses the text of the play established by R.A. Foakes in **The New Cambridge Shakespeare**.

The problem

At the court, Hippolyta and Duke Theseus are anticipating their marriage. Their plans are interrupted by Egeus, who is having a problem with his daughter Hermia. He wants to marry her to Demetrius. She is not co-operating because she is in love with Lysander.

The 'course of true love never did run smooth' Lysander and Hermia plan to meet in the wood at night, elope and marry. Will this solve the problem, or will the jealousy of Demetrius and his ex-love Helena spoil everything?

The fairies

'Ill met by moonlight, proud Titania!' The wood is the domain of the fairies ruled by Oberon and Titania. These powerful beings are in conflict, and their jealousies are causing a rift in both their relationship and the natural world.

It is in this stormy, unpredictable and magical place that the lovers decide to meet. The worlds of the fairies and the mortals are about to collide.

The mechanicals

'What hempen homespuns have we swaggering here . . . ?' The Mechanicals are rehearsing a play in the wood. They are ordinary men, not used to acting. Puck, Oberon's fairy servant, does not think much of them. He mischievously puts an ass's head on Bottom.

Oberon and Puck: '. . . make or man or woman madly dote / Upon the next live creature that it sees'. Oberon plans to use a magic love potion on Titania: 'What thou seest when thou dost wake, / Do it for thy true love take . . .'.

The potion – Bottom and Titania

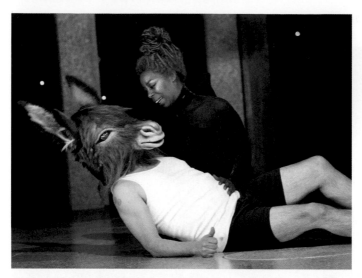

'O, how I love thee! How I dote on thee!' Newly 'translated' into an ass, Bottom sings to raise his spirits. His awful voice wakes Titania, who falls in love with him. These images show how two productions have presented this famously comic and yet poignant relationship.

The potion – The lovers

In attempting to sort out the lovers' tangle with the magic potion, Puck inadvertently makes things worse. Scenes of jealousy, abuse and rage ensue.

'Lord, what fools these mortals be!' Directors often make the most of the confusion, anger and hurt to present a crazy world with love gone badly wrong.

All wake up, happily ever after

All love problems are magically resolved. 'Are you sure / That we are awake? It seems to me / That yet we sleep, we dream.' Hermia and Lysander, Demetrius and Helena, Theseus and Hippolyta are all to marry.

'My Oberon, what visions have I seen!' Titania's love for Oberon returns.

The performance and wedding

The Mechanicals perform their play with all the seriousness of amateur theatricals. Their play is often funny, sad and surreal. This scene provides an opportunity for real slapstick humour.

'This is the silliest stuff that ever I heard.' The audience of newly-weds watch the Mechanicals' performance, wide eyed with disbelief.

The resolution and blessing

'To the best bride-bed will we, / Which by us shall blessèd be'. The three couples retire to bed at the end of their wedding day. Oberon and Titania bless the couples with loving marriages and perfect children.

'Give me your hands, if we be friends, / And Robin shall restore amends.' Shakespeare gives Puck the final word. He asks for a round of applause.

List of characters

The court
HIPPOLYTA queen of the Amazons, engaged to Theseus
THESEUS duke of Athens, engaged to Hippolyta
EGEUS father of Hermia
PHILOSTRATE master of the revels to the Athenian court

The lovers
HERMIA in love with Lysander
HELENA in love with Demetrius
LYSANDER in love with Hermia
DEMETRIUS Egeus' choice as a husband for Hermia

The Mechanicals
(workers who put on a play)
NICK BOTTOM a weaver who plays Pyramus
PETER QUINCE a carpenter who speaks the Prologue
FRANCIS FLUTE a bellows-mender who plays Thisbe
TOM SNOUT a tinker who plays Wall
ROBIN STARVELING a tailor who plays Moonshine
SNUG a joiner who plays Lion

The fairies
PUCK (or Robin Goodfellow) Oberon's attendant
OBERON king of the fairies
TITANIA queen of the fairies
PEASEBLOSSOM
COBWEB
MOTH } Titania's fairy attendants
MUSTARDSEED
A FAIRY in Titania's service

Hippolyta and Theseus have been at war and are now to marry to cement the new-found peace. Theseus regrets that time is moving slowly before he can marry Hippolyta. She says the four days will quickly pass. Theseus orders preparations for their wedding.

---

1 Theseus and Hippolyta – relationship? (in pairs)

Shakespeare chooses to use characters from a myth well known in his day. In the myth, Theseus, the duke of Athens, fought a battle with the Amazons (a group of warrior women) and then married Hippolyta, their queen. Taking parts, read lines 1–19 aloud, perhaps more than once. Then talk about what sort of relationship this seems to be.

2 Key words and images (in pairs)

Write down key words and images in lines 1–19 and look for patterns (like all those to do with the moon, or 'slow' versus 'quickly'). These patterns and the relationship between Theseus and Hippolyta give an idea of what the play will be about. Try to guess what might happen, and then share your ideas with another pair.

3 Fit actions to words (in groups of four)

Taking parts (with one person as Philostrate and one as director/ audience), walk through this opening, trying to develop gestures and movements that fit the speeches. Try making one partner dominant and the other quiet (or even resentful). Have them in love and affec- tionate. Think carefully about positioning and body language. Discuss which you like best, and why.

4 Moon, night and dreams

Think about the title of the play and the first speeches. Make notes on the kind of dream this play could be (a dream for the characters, or for the audience, or . . .)?

---

nuptial hour wedding time
step-dame stepmother
dowager a widow with money or
 property
revenue wealth

steep swallow, absorb
solemnities formal ceremonies
pale companion moon
pomp celebration
revelling merry-making

A Midsummer Night's Dream

Act 1 Scene 1
Athens Theseus' Palace

Enter THESEUS, HIPPOLYTA, PHILOSTRATE, *with others.*

THESEUS Now, fair Hippolyta, our nuptial hour
    Draws on apace; four happy days bring in
    Another moon – but O, methinks, how slow
    This old moon wanes! She lingers my desires,
    Like to a step-dame or a dowager   5
    Long withering out a young man's revenue.
HIPPOLYTA Four days will quickly steep themselves in night;
    Four nights will quickly dream away the time;
    And then the moon, like to a silver bow
    New bent in heaven, shall behold the night   10
    Of our solemnities.
THESEUS   Go, Philostrate,
    Stir up the Athenian youth to merriments,
    Awake the pert and nimble spirit of mirth;
    Turn melancholy forth to funerals;
    The pale companion is not for our pomp.   15
                               [Exit Philostrate]

    Hippolyta, I wooed thee with my sword,
    And won thy love doing thee injuries;
    But I will wed thee in another key,
    With pomp, with triumph, and with revelling.

Egeus enters with his daughter Hermia and the two men who wish to marry her, Lysander (whom she loves) and Demetrius (whom she dislikes). Egeus claims Lysander has 'bewitched' Hermia. He appeals to Theseus to support his right to decide whom his daughter marries.

1 What kind of father? (in groups of four)

Is Egeus being totally unreasonable, or is he a responsible Athenian father? Let one member of your group be Egeus and the others a 'court'. Ask Egeus questions and let him explain and defend what he says in lines 22–45.

Hippolyta does not speak during Egeus's 'complaint' or Theseus's response, yet her expression here speaks volumes. What is she thinking? Prepare her thoughts in note form. Then practise these ideas as a monologue. You may like to voice them in character to the class or straight to camera.

---

feigning untrue, deceitful
gauds, conceits fancy trinkets
Knacks knick-knacks
nosegays posies of flowers

sweetmeats sweets, candies
prevailment pressure
filched stolen

Enter EGEUS *and his daughter* HERMIA, LYSANDER *and* DEMETRIUS.

EGEUS Happy be Theseus, our renownèd Duke!   20
THESEUS Thanks, good Egeus. What's the news with thee?
EGEUS Full of vexation come I, with complaint
        Against my child, my daughter Hermia.
        Stand forth, Demetrius! – My noble lord,
        This man hath my consent to marry her.   25
        Stand forth, Lysander! – And, my gracious Duke,
        This man hath bewitched the bosom of my child.
        Thou, thou, Lysander, thou hast given her rhymes,
        And interchanged love-tokens with my child.
        Thou hast by moonlight at her window sung   30
        With feigning voice verses of feigning love,
        And stolen the impression of her fantasy,
        With bracelets of thy hair, rings, gauds, conceits,
        Knacks, trifles, nosegays, sweetmeats – messengers
        Of strong prevailment in unhardened youth;   35
        With cunning hast thou filched my daughter's heart,
        Turned her obedience, which is due to me,
        To stubborn harshness. And, my gracious Duke,
        Be it so she will not here, before your grace,
        Consent to marry with Demetrius,   40
        I beg the ancient privilege of Athens;
        As she is mine, I may dispose of her;
        Which shall be either to this gentleman
        Or to her death, according to our law
        Immediately provided in that case.   45

Hermia pleads to be allowed to choose Lysander for a husband. Theseus warns her to abide by Egeus's decision, otherwise she risks being sent to a convent or to her death.

---

1 Parents versus children (in groups of four)

Discuss Theseus's views, and consider what children owe their parents. Make a list of the advantages and disadvantages of arranged marriages.

Hermia (kneeling) pleads while Hippolyta looks on.

2 Sisterhood

On this page Hermia stands up for herself as a lone female figure on the stage, surrounded by squabbling men. However, Hippolyta says nothing. Why? What is she thinking? Shakespeare has decided to leave her silent. Decide whether, as director, you would have some recognition pass between Hermia and Hippolyta, and, if so, suggest how it would be done.

---

imprinted moulded, stamped
wanting not having
blood feelings
aye ever
mewed confined

barren sister nun
distilled made into perfume
unwishèd yoke unwanted constraint
sovereignty power, control

THESEUS What say you, Hermia? Be advised, fair maid.
　　　　To you your father should be as a god,
　　　　One that composed your beauties; yea, and one
　　　　To whom you are but as a form in wax
　　　　By him imprinted, and within his power　　　　　　　　　　50
　　　　To leave the figure, or disfigure it.
　　　　Demetrius is a worthy gentleman.
HERMIA So is Lysander.
THESEUS　　　　　　　　In himself he is;
　　　　But in this kind, wanting your father's voice,
　　　　The other must be held the worthier.　　　　　　　　　55
HERMIA I would my father looked but with my eyes.
THESEUS Rather your eyes must with his judgement look.
HERMIA I do entreat your grace to pardon me.
　　　　I know not by what power I am made bold,
　　　　Nor how it may concern my modesty　　　　　　　　　60
　　　　In such a presence here to plead my thoughts;
　　　　But I beseech your grace that I may know
　　　　The worst that may befall me in this case,
　　　　If I refuse to wed Demetrius.
THESEUS Either to die the death, or to abjure　　　　　　　　65
　　　　For ever the society of men.
　　　　Therefore, fair Hermia, question your desires,
　　　　Know of your youth, examine well your blood,
　　　　Whether, if you yield not to your father's choice,
　　　　You can endure the livery of a nun,　　　　　　　　　70
　　　　For aye to be in shady cloister mewed,
　　　　To live a barren sister all your life,
　　　　Chanting faint hymns to the cold fruitless moon.
　　　　Thrice blessèd they that master so their blood
　　　　To undergo such maiden pilgrimage;　　　　　　　　　75
　　　　But earthlier happy is the rose distilled
　　　　Than that which, withering on the virgin thorn,
　　　　Grows, lives, and dies in single blessedness.
HERMIA So will I grow, so live, so die, my lord,
　　　　Ere I will yield my virgin patent up　　　　　　　　　80
　　　　Unto his lordship, whose unwishèd yoke
　　　　My soul consents not to give sovereignty.

Theseus orders Hermia to make her decision before his wedding to Hippolyta. Lysander argues his case and points out that Demetrius loved Helena before Hermia, and that Helena still loves him.

---

1 Hermia's dilemma – what would you do?

Would you rather die or be imprisoned than marry someone you disliked? (Assume there is no possibility of divorce.) Give reasons for your reply.

2 '. . . looked but with my eyes' (in pairs or threes)

In line 56, Hermia means she wishes that Egeus could 'see' Lysander as she sees him. The people watching 'see' the debates in lines 46–110 very differently. Discuss what each character sees and why.

3 Male dominance (in groups of four)

Already there has been a 'forced' engagement. Go through lines 36–110, finding any images that imply male dominance – for example, 'your father should be as a god'. Read the images about males, then those about females, and say which you find acceptable and which you find offensive – and why.

4 'Love' and 'dote' (in groups of four)

From line 46, there is a good deal of talk about feelings. Try to identify these different feelings and explain what they are. Talk together about which characters are sensitive to others' feelings, and which are not. Begin to compile a list of all the words and phrases so far which describe or explore emotion. When you reach the end of Act 1, group them in a way which you think makes sense. Make a display, perhaps with pictures.

---

sealing-day wedding day
austerity self-control, abstinence
estate unto give to
as well-derived of as good a family and background

well-possessed rich
with vantage rather better
avouch guarantee, swear
to his head to his face

THESEUS Take time to pause, and by the next new moon,
      The sealing-day betwixt my love and me
      For everlasting bond of fellowship, 85
      Upon that day either prepare to die
      For disobedience to your father's will,
      Or else to wed Demetrius, as he would,
      Or on Diana's altar to protest
      For aye austerity and single life. 90
DEMETRIUS Relent, sweet Hermia; and, Lysander, yield
      Thy crazèd title to my certain right.
LYSANDER You have her father's love, Demetrius;
      Let me have Hermia's – do you marry him.
EGEUS Scornful Lysander, true, he hath my love, 95
      And what is mine my love shall render him;
      And she is mine, and all my right of her
      I do estate unto Demetrius.
LYSANDER I am, my lord, as well-derived as he,
      As well-possessed: my love is more than his, 100
      My fortunes every way as fairly ranked,
      If not with vantage, as Demetrius';
      And, which is more than all these boasts can be,
      I am beloved of beauteous Hermia.
      Why should not I then prosecute my right? 105
      Demetrius, I'll avouch it to his head,
      Made love to Nedar's daughter, Helena,
      And won her soul; and she, sweet lady, dotes,
      Devoutly dotes, dotes in idolatry,
      Upon this spotted and inconstant man. 110

With a final warning to Hermia, Theseus takes Demetrius and Egeus away to talk to them. Left alone, Lysander and Hermia lament the problems of lovers.

1 Hippolyta speaks her mind (in pairs)

Hippolyta and Theseus leave together. They will shortly be married. Improvise the conversation they may have about what has just happened, what each thinks of the situation and the characters involved. Bear in mind how Hippolyta might relate to Hermia's plight and Theseus's judgement. Use clues from the script as much as you can. Remember that she was 'wooed' with a sword. When Theseus says 'what cheer, my love?' what does it imply?

2 Love, 'short as any dream' – is it? (in pairs)

In lines 141–9, Lysander paints love as a temporary thing: 'momentany' (momentary), 'Swift', 'short', 'Brief', surrounded by a hostile world. Talk about what he compares love to, and whether you think the comparisons are suitable.

3 'The course of true love never did run smooth'

Line 134 has become a commonplace saying. How true is it? Think about what it might imply about the rest of the play. Make a list of films and TV serials which use this saying as a theme.

4 The dance of the lovers – who loves whom? (I)

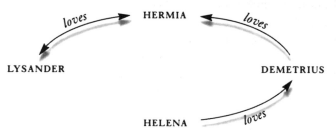

---

extenuate change, reduce	**misgraffèd** mismatched
Against in preparation for	**momentany** momentary
Beteem grant	**collied** darkened, like coal
blood class, family background	**spleen** burst of temper
enthralled bound	

THESEUS I must confess that I have heard so much,
And with Demetrius thought to have spoke thereof;
But, being overfull of self-affairs,
My mind did lose it. But Demetrius, come,
And come, Egeus. You shall go with me;   115
I have some private schooling for you both.
For you, fair Hermia, look you arm yourself
To fit your fancies to your father's will;
Or else the law of Athens yields you up
(Which by no means we may extenuate)   120
To death, or to a vow of single life.
Come, my Hippolyta; what cheer, my love?
Demetrius and Egeus, go along;
I must employ you in some business
Against our nuptial, and confer with you   125
Of something nearly that concerns yourselves.

EGEUS With duty and desire we follow you.

                    Exeunt all but Lysander and Hermia

LYSANDER How now, my love? Why is your cheek so pale?
How chance the roses there do fade so fast?

HERMIA Belike for want of rain, which I could well   130
Beteem them from the tempest of my eyes.

LYSANDER Ay me! For aught that I could ever read,
Could ever hear by tale or history,
The course of true love never did run smooth;
But either it was different in blood –   135

HERMIA O cross! too high to be enthralled to low.

LYSANDER Or else misgraffèd in respect of years –

HERMIA O spite! too old to be engaged to young.

LYSANDER Or else it stood upon the choice of friends –

HERMIA O hell, to choose love by another's eyes!   140

LYSANDER Or, if there were a sympathy in choice,
War, death, or sickness did lay siege to it,
Making it momentany as a sound,
Swift as a shadow, short as any dream,
Brief as the lightning in the collied night,   145
That in a spleen unfolds both heaven and earth,
And, ere a man hath power to say 'Behold!',
The jaws of darkness do devour it up.
So quick bright things come to confusion.

Lysander and Hermia plan to elope: to run away to Lysander's widowed aunt who lives beyond the reach of the Athenian law. They arrange to meet 'tomorrow night' in the wood outside the city.

1 Running away – is it sensible? (in small groups)

Begin by talking about running away from problems and running away as a couple. Is it ever a wise move? Consider Lysander and Hermia's situation and list the different options the lovers have and which is wisest. Plot a storyboard which presents a modern-day dilemma which might be resolved (could be sorted out) by running away.

2 From patience to enthusiasm (in pairs)

Hermia suggests (line 152) that they be patient, and Lysander agrees ('A good persuasion'), but then he suggests they run away. Hermia immediately assents. To experience Hermia's resolve to be patient, then how she is persuaded, take parts and speak lines 150–79. Make Lysander very persuasive, and show how Hermia responds whole-heartedly.

3 How old?

Because of their behaviour, perhaps Shakespeare is suggesting that the lovers are very young. Suggest how old you think Hermia, Lysander and Demetrius are. Consequently, how old are Theseus and Hippolyta? Give reasons for your opinions.

4 What do lovers dream? (in small groups)

Hermia speaks of features of love ('fancy's followers') like thoughts and wishes and dreams. Talk about what sort of dreams lovers have (being together, freedom from restrictions, happiness, sex . . .). She also swears oaths by the goddess of love (Venus) and other lovers (Dido, queen of Carthage, who loved Aeneas, the false Trojan). Love, for Hermia, is like a dream she lives in all the time. Is this what love is like? Discuss whether you think that people in love are inhabiting a dream world.

---

edict command
persuasion doctrine, set of principles
revenue wealth

leagues (a league is about three miles)
do observance celebrate

HERMIA If then true lovers have been ever crossed   150
        It stands as an edict in destiny.
        Then let us teach our trial patience,
        Because it is a customary cross,
        As due to love as thoughts, and dreams, and sighs,
        Wishes, and tears – poor fancy's followers.   155
LYSANDER A good persuasion. Therefore hear me, Hermia:
        I have a widow aunt, a dowager,
        Of great revenue, and she hath no child.
        From Athens is her house remote seven leagues;
        And she respects me as her only son.   160
        There, gentle Hermia, may I marry thee;
        And to that place the sharp Athenian law
        Cannot pursue us. If thou lov'st me, then
        Steal forth thy father's house tomorrow night,
        And in the wood, a league without the town   165
        (Where I did meet thee once with Helena
        To do observance to a morn of May),
        There will I stay for thee.
HERMIA   My good Lysander,
        I swear to thee by Cupid's strongest bow,
        By his best arrow with the golden head,   170
        By the simplicity of Venus' doves,
        By that which knitteth souls and prospers loves,
        And by that fire which burned the Carthage queen
        When the false Trojan under sail was seen,
        By all the vows that ever men have broke   175
        (In number more than ever women spoke),
        In that same place thou hast appointed me,
        Tomorrow truly will I meet with thee.
LYSANDER Keep promise, love. Look, here comes Helena.

Helena enters and talks of Demetrius's love for Hermia. She wishes she were like Hermia. To console her, Hermia and Lysander tell her of their plan to elope.

1 What do you make of Helena? (in pairs)

Read through Helena and Hermia's lines 180–207, then talk about Helena and her situation. Identify key words and phrases that bring out her character. Read these aloud, or act out the lines emphasising those key words and phrases. What is your impression of Helena?

2 How might it end? (in groups of four)

Shakespeare has set up an extremely difficult situation for his lovers (remember that Helena is in love too, even if her love is not returned). If the play is a comedy, in the sense that there is a happy ending for all the lovers, it's a bit hard to see how it will happen. Invent a variety of different plots that might bring them together at the end.

3 Patterns of language (in pairs)

Poetry is a kind of patterned speech or writing. You've probably noticed how the play is in blank verse and rhyming couplets so far (even if you didn't know the names of this kind of poetry). Shakespeare also uses other patterns. Speak lines 194–201 to each other, then say what kinds of pattern you find in this conversation (there is help on pp. 164–5).

4 'Seemed Athens as a paradise to me'

Hermia says her feelings for Athens have completely changed (line 205). From what you know so far, what kind of place do you think Athens is? How does it compare to the world you live in?

Whither away? Where are you going?
fair beautiful
lodestars guiding stars
favour appearance

bated excepted
Phoebe Diana, goddess of the moon, associated with chastity

Enter HELENA.

HERMIA   God speed, fair Helena! Whither away?   180
HELENA   Call you me fair? That 'fair' again unsay.
         Demetrius loves your fair: O happy fair!
         Your eyes are lodestars, and your tongue's sweet air
         More tuneable than lark to shepherd's ear
         When wheat is green, when hawthorn buds appear.   185
         Sickness is catching. O, were favour so,
         Yours would I catch, fair Hermia, ere I go;
         My ear should catch your voice, my eye your eye,
         My tongue should catch your tongue's sweet melody.
         Were the world mine, Demetrius being bated,   190
         The rest I'd give to be to you translated.
         O, teach me how you look, and with what art
         You sway the motion of Demetrius' heart.
HERMIA   I frown upon him; yet he loves me still.
HELENA   O that your frowns would teach my smiles such skill!   195
HERMIA   I give him curses; yet he gives me love.
HELENA   O that my prayers could such affection move!
HERMIA   The more I hate, the more he follows me.
HELENA   The more I love, the more he hateth me.
HERMIA   His folly, Helena, is no fault of mine.   200
HELENA   None but your beauty; would that fault were mine!
HERMIA   Take comfort: he no more shall see my face;
         Lysander and myself will fly this place.
         Before the time I did Lysander see,
         Seemed Athens as a paradise to me.   205
         O then, what graces in my love do dwell,
         That he hath turned a heaven unto a hell?
LYSANDER Helen, to you our minds we will unfold:
         Tomorrow night, when Phoebe doth behold
         Her silver visage in the watery glass,   210
         Decking with liquid pearl the bladed grass
         (A time that lovers' flights doth still conceal),
         Through Athens' gates have we devised to steal.

Hermia and Lysander leave, wishing Helena luck with Demetrius. Helena reflects on the transforming and deceiving nature of love, and decides to tell Demetrius of the elopement in order to win his thanks.

---

1 Your view of the lovers (in groups of four)

This scene ends with Helena's decision to tell Demetrius about the elopement. Discuss the four lovers separately, saying what you think of each. Think in terms of the different relationships (Hermia and Helena, Hermia and Demetrius and so on). How are they different, or the same; which do you like best (and least)?

Work out a typical pose for each character which sums up your perception of them. Take a photograph if you can, perhaps with a speech bubble added.

2 Past events – two activities (in groups of four)

a Hermia talks of her past times with Helena ('where often you and I . . .'). Imagine what might have occurred in the past two months leading up to this scene – meetings between any of the lovers, incidents, conversations or arguments, and so on. Pick one and improvise it. Show it to the class.

b What does exploring their past in this way add to the audience's understanding of their present? Tell other group members how it helps your understanding of character and how it influences your feelings for them.

3 Love – 'winged Cupid' – Helena's view (in pairs)

Helena explains what she thinks of love in lines 232–9, using a comparison with Cupid (the mythical god of love, a young child with wings, who was sometimes presented as being blind). Work carefully through these lines, two lines at a time, until you're sure of what she's saying (ask for help if you need it). Discuss Helena's view of love. Is it true of lovers you know?

---

were wont used
holding no quantity having no value
figure suggest
beguiled tricked
waggish mischievous

forswear falsely promise
ere before
eyne eyes
intelligence information

HERMIA And in the wood, where often you and I
　　　　Upon faint primrose beds were wont to lie,　　　　215
　　　　Emptying our bosoms of their counsel sweet,
　　　　There my Lysander and myself shall meet,
　　　　And thence from Athens turn away our eyes
　　　　To seek new friends and stranger companies.
　　　　Farewell, sweet playfellow; pray thou for us,　　　　220
　　　　And good luck grant thee thy Demetrius.
　　　　Keep word, Lysander; we must starve our sight
　　　　From lovers' food till morrow deep midnight.
LYSANDER I will, my Hermia.

　　　　　　　　　　　　　　　　　　Exit Hermia

　　　　　　　Helena, adieu!
　　　　As you on him, Demetrius dote on you.　　*Exit Lysander*　225
HELENA How happy some o'er other some can be!
　　　　Through Athens I am thought as fair as she.
　　　　But what of that? Demetrius thinks not so;
　　　　He will not know what all but he do know.
　　　　And as he errs, doting on Hermia's eyes,　　　　230
　　　　So I, admiring of his qualities.
　　　　Things base and vile, holding no quantity,
　　　　Love can transpose to form and dignity.
　　　　Love looks not with the eyes, but with the mind,
　　　　And therefore is winged Cupid painted blind.　　　　235
　　　　Nor hath love's mind of any judgement taste;
　　　　Wings, and no eyes, figure unheedy haste;
　　　　And therefore is love said to be a child
　　　　Because in choice he is so oft beguiled.
　　　　As waggish boys in game themselves forswear,　　　　240
　　　　So the boy Love is perjured everywhere;
　　　　For, ere Demetrius looked on Hermia's eyne,
　　　　He hailed down oaths that he was only mine,
　　　　And when this hail some heat from Hermia felt,
　　　　So he dissolved, and showers of oaths did melt.　　　　245
　　　　I will go tell him of fair Hermia's flight:
　　　　Then to the wood will he, tomorrow night,
　　　　Pursue her; and for this intelligence,
　　　　If I have thanks it is a dear expense;
　　　　But herein mean I to enrich my pain,　　　　250
　　　　To have his sight thither, and back again.　　*Exit*

A group of workers (the Mechanicals) – Quince, Snug, Bottom, Flute, Snout and Starveling – meet to allocate the parts for a play, which they hope to perform at the duke's wedding.

1 Who have we here? (in groups of six)

a To gain a first impression, take parts and speak the whole scene. Then work on one or more of the following.

b Shakespeare gives these characters distinctive names and trades. Consider how the name and trade of each helps establish character. Choose a character, and work for a little while on your own, reading your character's lines and thinking about how to develop your part. Come back together to act out this scene. You might like to keep together as a team for the Mechanicals' sections of the play.

c The Mechanicals are a distinct group of characters, yet each is an individual. Look at the photos of the Mechanicals in the colour section and on other pages. How would you want your Mechanicals to appear physically? Think in terms of colours, costumes and physical and verbal mannerisms that would make them stand out as individuals for an audience but remain part of a group.

d The Mechanicals are a real contrast with the mythical court of Athens, if only because they are so clearly of Shakespeare's time and place. Talk about the differences between the court and the workmen, and why Shakespeare might have included the Mechanicals and their very different world.

e Everyone knows a Bottom-like character – perhaps there is even one in your group. Talk about what you think of Bottom (and what the other Mechanicals think of him). He is one of the most popular of all Shakespeare's characters, despite being so completely over the top – why might this be? Do you think Shakespeare intended the audience to be laughing with him – or at him?

---

interlude play
lamentable sad, distressing
spread yourselves spread out
condole show grief
Ercles Hercules

to tear a cat in to rant and rave. What kind of acting is Bottom used to, and what kind of play?
Phibbus Phoebus, god of the sun, who was supposed to drive a chariot ('car') through the sky

Act 1 Scene 2
Athens

Enter QUINCE the Carpenter, and SNUG the Joiner, and BOTTOM
the Weaver, and FLUTE the Bellows-mender, and SNOUT the
Tinker and STARVELING the Tailor.

QUINCE Is all our company here?

BOTTOM You were best to call them generally, man by man, according
to the scrip.

QUINCE Here is the scroll of every man's name which is thought fit
through all Athens to play in our interlude before the Duke and   5
the Duchess on his wedding day at night.

BOTTOM First, good Peter Quince, say what the play treats on; then
read the names of the actors; and so grow to a point.

QUINCE Marry, our play is 'The most lamentable comedy and most
cruel death of Pyramus and Thisbe'.   10

BOTTOM A very good piece of work, I assure you, and a merry. Now,
good Peter Quince, call forth your actors by the scroll. Masters,
spread yourselves.

QUINCE Answer as I call you. Nick Bottom, the weaver?

BOTTOM Ready. Name what part I am for, and proceed.   15

QUINCE You, Nick Bottom, are set down for Pyramus.

BOTTOM What is Pyramus? A lover or a tyrant?

QUINCE A lover that kills himself, most gallant, for love.

BOTTOM That will ask some tears in the true performing of it. If I do
it, let the audience look to their eyes: I will move storms, I will   20
condole, in some measure. To the rest – yet my chief humour is
for a tyrant. I could play Ercles rarely, or a part to tear a cat in,
to make all split:

> The raging rocks
> And shivering shocks   25
> Shall break the locks
>   Of prison gates,
> And Phibbus' car
> Shall shine from far,
> And make and mar   30
>   The foolish Fates.

Quince assigns parts to each of the Mechanicals. Bottom is enthusiastic and volunteers to play two roles, but Quince, who is to direct, says no.

1 Problems of playing (in groups of six)

a ' . . . a monstrous little voice' The problem of Flute playing a woman (lines 36–44) is partly solved, so the Mechanicals believe, by Flute speaking in a high-pitched voice. Discuss how each of the Mechanicals might speak normally, and then try out different voices for each (different accents and speed, and so on). For example, if Bottom is playing the play's hero, how would he try to talk, and how successful would he be?

b 'I have a beard coming' In one production Flute was played by a very young actor who had obviously not yet started shaving. He solved the problem of line 39, and gained a huge laugh from the audience, by saying 'I have a beard' and pausing. In the pause, all the Mechanicals stared at him in disbelief. Flute felt his chin, then added assertively, 'coming'. As you read on, look out for other unexpected ways of making the audience laugh.

c 'Let not me play a woman' On Shakespeare's stage, all the actors were male. Rehearse and act out this scene in which all the characters are male; and Act 1 Scene 1, lines 180–224, in which the characters are predominantly female. How do you feel about playing someone of the opposite sex? Identify the problems and opportunities it presents.

d ' . . . they would shriek' The Mechanicals seem to think that if Bottom played the lion's part he would frighten the women in the audience (lines 60–3). What does this tell you about the Mechanicals and the kinds of plays they might have seen?

Ercles' vein Hercules's style   **fitted** cast
small high pitched

This was lofty. Now name the rest of the players. – This is Ercles'
vein, a tyrant's vein; a lover is more condoling.

QUINCE Francis Flute, the bellows-mender?

FLUTE Here, Peter Quince.   35

QUINCE Flute, you must take Thisbe on you.

FLUTE What is Thisbe? A wandering knight?

QUINCE It is the lady that Pyramus must love.

FLUTE Nay, faith, let not me play a woman: I have a beard coming.

QUINCE That's all one: you shall play it in a mask, and you may speak   40
as small as you will.

BOTTOM And I may hide my face, let me play Thisbe too. I'll speak
in a monstrous little voice: 'Thisne, Thisne!' – 'Ah, Pyramus, my
lover dear; thy Thisbe dear, and lady dear.'

QUINCE No, no; you must play Pyramus; and Flute, you Thisbe.   45

BOTTOM Well, proceed.

QUINCE Robin Starveling, the tailor?

STARVELING Here, Peter Quince.

QUINCE Robin Starveling, you must play Thisbe's mother. Tom Snout,
the tinker?   50

SNOUT Here, Peter Quince.

QUINCE You, Pyramus' father; myself, Thisbe's father; Snug, the
joiner, you the lion's part; and I hope here is a play fitted.

Quince completes the arrangements for the play, despite Bottom's interruptions. They plan to meet in the wood 'tomorrow night' for a private rehearsal.

The Mechanicals. Choose a line as a suitable caption.

1 The Mechanicals' language (in pairs)

The Mechanicals' language is very different from that of the court characters. Make a list of contradictions, mistakes and odd things they say in Scene 2.

extempore ad lib
proper handsome
French-crown (sexually transmitted disease, leading to baldness)
con learn

be dogged with company have people watching
draw a bill of properties compile a list of props
be perfect know your lines perfectly

SNUG Have you the lion's part written? Pray you, if it be, give it me; for I am slow of study.   55

QUINCE You may do it extempore; for it is nothing but roaring.

BOTTOM Let me play the lion too. I will roar that I will do any man's heart good to hear me. I will roar that I will make the Duke say 'Let him roar again, let him roar again!'

QUINCE And you should do it too terribly, you would fright the   60 Duchess and the ladies that they would shriek; and that were enough to hang us all.

ALL That would hang us, every mother's son.

BOTTOM I grant you, friends, if you should fright the ladies out of their wits they would have no more discretion but to hang us; but I will   65 aggravate my voice so that I will roar you as gently as any sucking dove. I will roar you and 'twere any nightingale.

QUINCE You can play no part but Pyramus; for Pyramus is a sweet-faced man, a proper man as one shall see in a summer's day, a most lovely, gentlemanlike man: therefore you must needs play Pyramus.   70

BOTTOM Well, I will undertake it. What beard were I best to play it in?

QUINCE Why, what you will.

BOTTOM I will discharge it in either your straw-colour beard, your orange-tawny beard, your purple-in-grain beard, or your   75 French-crown-colour beard, your perfect yellow.

QUINCE Some of your French crowns have no hair at all, and then you will play bare-faced. But, masters, here are your parts, and I am to entreat you, request you, and desire you to con them by tomorrow night, and meet me in the palace wood, a mile without   80 the town, by moonlight; there will we rehearse, for if we meet in the city we shall be dogged with company, and our devices known. In the meantime I will draw a bill of properties, such as our play wants. I pray you, fail me not.

BOTTOM We will meet, and there we may rehearse most obscenely and   85 courageously. Take pains, be perfect: adieu!

QUINCE At the Duke's oak we meet.

BOTTOM Enough; hold, or cut bowstrings.

Exeunt

Looking back at Act 1
Activities for groups or individuals

1 Hippolyta – and Queen Elizabeth 1

The Hippolyta pictured here is dressed as Queen Elizabeth I, who was on the throne when this play was written. Elizabeth once famously said: 'I know I have the body of a weak and feeble woman, but I have the heart and stomach of a king . . .'.

Hippolyta is usually a dominant personage on stage, but she says very little. Write several paragraphs on how you interpret her character, and how a reminder of the times in which the play was written helps you with that interpretation.

2 More history – Bottom's version

The Mechanicals' fear of bringing on a lion may be based on an actual incident. Just before Shakespeare wrote the play, a lion was excluded from celebrations in the Scottish court because it 'might have brought some fear'. The story was well known. Imagine Bottom tells that tale to the others. Write him a speech of ten lines – in his own unique style.

3 Egeus: a bully, or . . .?

Egeus may appear simply as an egotistical bully. But he can be played to present a different impression from that. Try out some ideas.

4 Different versions of love

a *A Midsummer Night's Dream* is a play very much about love. But what is love? In one of the harsher moments in the play, Egeus describes love as 'feigning' and 'cunning' (Scene 1, lines 31 and 36). Talk together about 'love' and what you think it is. Identify the problems love can cause and what solutions there might be to these problems. Write down your ideas about love, and record other views of love as you come to them in the play.

b How do the lovers talk about love? Lysander says 'The course of true love never did run smooth'. Compare this to the Mechanicals' presentation of love and the views of the court characters. If you were directing, how would you bring out the links between these ideas for the audience?

5 Word pictures – verbal imagery

The words characters speak often create 'word pictures', or images in your imagination. Some phrases conjure up clear visual pictures in your mind's eye ('Chanting faint hymns to the cold fruitless moon'). Other expressions are more complex and are difficult to visualise ('Swift as a shadow, short as any dream'). Like every image on stage, all word images can communicate a great deal to your imaginative understanding of the play. Choose a short passage (e.g. Scene 1, lines 214–23), and talk together about the images called up in your mind. 'Imagery' on pages 161–4 will help you.

6 Stage pictures – visual imagery

A play combines verbal imagery with visual images (e.g. the actors' gestures and actions). Sometimes the visual images match the verbal imagery. For example, when in Act 2 Puck says 'I'll put a girdle round about the earth', what gesture might he make to express the image physically? Pick a short passage from Act 1 and rehearse it. Act it without words (mime it), and then just read the words aloud. Discuss what you find. Do the words match your 'pictures'?

A fairy in the service of Titania, queen of the fairies, meets Puck. Puck explains the conflict over an Indian boy between Oberon, the king of the fairies, and Titania.

1 Introducing the fairy world (in pairs)

One of Shakespeare's favourite dramatic techniques is to contrast scene with scene. Here, after presenting the worlds of the court and the Mechanicals to the audience, he introduces a third world: the fairy kingdom. Try some or all of the following activities to gain a first impression of the fairy world.

a **Mind movie** Relax and close your eyes as your teacher reads the poetry (lines 2–31) aloud to you. Imagine this world as vividly as you can. Share your picture with a partner.

b **Comparisons and contrasts** Compare and contrast this fairy world with the two worlds of the first act. Make brief notes to identify the similarities and differences such as the love conflict, styles of speaking and so on.

c **Act it out!** Act lines 1–31, using gestures and movements that bring out the world of fairies as you think it should be. Think about how the fairies would move and speak differently from the court characters and the Mechanicals.

2 What does the audience see? (in groups of four)

Both speeches opposite create visions (or dreams) in the audience's mind of things that happen in the fairy world. Some images would be very difficult to put a stage (e.g. 'elves for fear / Creep into acorn cups'). Discuss how much help the audience needs to imagine what is described (this scene is set at night in a wood). You could be like the Mechanicals – very literal in trying to present everything – or leave it all to the power of Shakespeare's language.

---

thorough through
orbs fairy rings
savours scent
lob lout
anon soon

passing . . . wrath very fierce and angry
changeling a child stolen by fairies
starlight sheen shining starlight
square quarrel

Act 2 Scene 1
The wood

Enter a FAIRY at one door, and PUCK, or ROBIN GOODFELLOW
at another.

PUCK How now, spirit; whither wander you?

FAIRY   Over hill, over dale,
         Thorough bush, thorough briar,
       Over park, over pale,
         Thorough flood, thorough fire;   5
       I do wander everywhere
       Swifter than the moon's sphere;
       And I serve the Fairy Queen,
       To dew her orbs upon the green.
       The cowslips tall her pensioners be;   10
       In their gold coats spots you see –
       Those be rubies, fairy favours,
       In those freckles live their savours.
         I must go seek some dewdrops here,
         And hang a pearl in every cowslip's ear.   15
     Farewell, thou lob of spirits; I'll be gone.
     Our Queen and all her elves come here anon.

PUCK The King doth keep his revels here tonight.
     Take heed the Queen come not within his sight,
     For Oberon is passing fell and wrath,   20
     Because that she as her attendant hath
     A lovely boy stol'n from an Indian king;
     She never had so sweet a changeling,
     And jealous Oberon would have the child
     Knight of his train, to trace the forests wild.   25
     But she perforce withholds the lovèd boy,
     Crowns him with flowers, and makes him all her joy.
     And now they never meet in grove or green,
     By fountain clear or spangled starlight sheen,
     But they do square, that all their elves for fear   30
     Creep into acorn cups and hide them there.

Puck and the fairy talk about the sort of 'sprite' Puck is. In both descriptions he is mischievous and plays tricks.

---

1 Puck – or Robin Goodfellow: what is he like?

Puck is one of Shakespeare's best-known characters, and both speeches opposite introduce him to the audience. Make a list of the adjectives used to describe him ('shrewd', and so on), and a list of what he is described as doing. Using both lists, describe what kind of character he is. Add to your lists as you read on.

2 Fit actions to the words (in pairs)

Take turns reading Puck's speech (lines 43–58) and fit actions to it, miming some of the things he talks about.

3 What do you see? (in small groups)

Look at the presentations of Puck in the colour section and elsewhere in this edition. Discuss each one, commenting on why Puck looks the way he does. Do any surprise you?

4 Characters from myth and legend

This quotation comes from a book Shakespeare probably read, called *The Discovery of Witchcraft*, which was written in 1584:

> Indeed your grandams' maids set a bowl of milk out for Robin Goodfellow . . . the mare, the man in the oak, the puckle, hobgoblin.

The book describes incidents similar to those the fairy and Puck talk about, but, as the quotation implies, hardly anyone believed in Puck or Robin Goodfellow any more. Think about why Shakespeare uses so many imaginary characters from myth and superstition in this particular play.

---

shrewd evil or mischievous. Which do you think suits him best: this or Puck's own description of himself?
knavish roguish, unprincipled
Skim milk skim off the cream
quern hand mill for grinding corn

bootless pointless
barm head (on beer)
crab crab apple
dewlap hanging, loose skin on the neck
loffe laugh

FAIRY Either I mistake your shape and making quite,
Or else you are that shrewd and knavish sprite
Called Robin Goodfellow. Are not you he
That frights the maidens of the villagery,   35
Skim milk, and sometimes labour in the quern,
And bootless make the breathless housewife churn,
And sometime make the drink to bear no barm,
Mislead night-wanderers, laughing at their harm?
Those that 'Hobgoblin' call you, and 'Sweet Puck',   40
You do their work, and they shall have good luck.
Are not you he?

PUCK   Thou speakest aright;
I am that merry wanderer of the night.
I jest to Oberon, and make him smile
When I a fat and bean-fed horse beguile,   45
Neighing in likeness of a filly foal;
And sometime lurk I in a gossip's bowl
In very likeness of a roasted crab,
And when she drinks, against her lips I bob,
And on her withered dewlap pour the ale.   50
The wisest aunt, telling the saddest tale,
Sometime for threefoot stool mistaketh me;
Then slip I from her bum, down topples she,
And 'Tailor' cries, and falls into a cough;
And then the whole choir hold their hips and loffe,   55
And waxen in their mirth, and neeze, and swear
A merrier hour was never wasted there.
But room, Fairy: here comes Oberon.

FAIRY And here my mistress. Would that he were gone!

Oberon and Titania enter with their attendants. They accuse each other of being attracted to the mortals Theseus and Hippolyta.

In many ways, what a play looks like is as important as what is said. Discuss what this photograph says ('What's going on?' is a good starting point). Compare it with other fairy photographs in the colour section and on pages 42, 44, 66, 100, 152 and 170.

train attendants	**buskined** wearing hunting boots
Tarry wait	**Perigenia, Aegles, Ariadne,**
lord, lady (they are husband and wife)	**Antiopa** women Theseus slept
Corin, Phillida two mythical lovers	with

Enter [OBERON,] *the King of Fairies, at one door, with his train; and*
[TITANIA,] *the Queen, at another with hers.*

OBERON	Ill met by moonlight, proud Titania!	60
TITANIA	What, jealous Oberon? Fairies, skip hence.	
	I have forsworn his bed and company.	
OBERON	Tarry, rash wanton! Am not I thy lord?	
TITANIA	Then I must be thy lady. But I know	
	When thou hast stol'n away from Fairyland,	65
	And in the shape of Corin sat all day	
	Playing on pipes of corn, and versing love	
	To amorous Phillida. Why art thou here	
	Come from the farthest step of India? –	
	But that, forsooth, the bouncing Amazon,	70
	Your buskined mistress and your warrior love,	
	To Theseus must be wedded; and you come	
	To give their bed joy and prosperity.	
OBERON	How canst thou thus, for shame, Titania,	
	Glance at my credit with Hippolyta,	75
	Knowing I know thy love to Theseus?	
	Didst not thou lead him through the glimmering night	
	From Perigenia, whom he ravishèd,	
	And make him with fair Aegles break his faith,	
	With Ariadne, and Antiopa?	80

Titania claims that the dispute with Oberon has changed the natural patterns of the climate and the seasons.

---

1 Changing world – changing language (in pairs)

Our world is always changing, and so is our language. You can see some of these changes by comparing Shakespeare's language with the way we speak and write today. Use Titania's lines 81–117 to look for evidence of an older way of life ('ox . . . stretched his yoke') and beliefs ('Contagious fogs'). You can see how writing about an older way of life means using different language. Then identify words no longer used today. Finally, look for uses of language that are distinctive because this is poetry. Titania describes the disruption of the natural world because of the conflict between her and Oberon (this suggests their power in and over nature). Write another speech (in prose or in verse) about a similar problem of today – global warming. Relate it to stormy emotions. Use contemporary imagery, and compare your use of language with Shakespeare's.

2 Relationships: fairy world, court world (in small groups)

Discuss the relationship between Titania and Oberon as shown in lines 60–117, and the sexual nature of their conversation. This is another conflict between lovers. Talk together about parallels with the relationships in the first act, and what sort of mood it creates here. Then discuss what lines 115–17 imply about the importance of Oberon and Titania's relationship.

3 'These are the forgeries of jealousy'

Make a collage of the images in this speech. 'Imagery' (pp. 161–4) will help you.

---

forgeries lies
beachèd margent shore
ringlets dancing in a circle
brawls quarrels
murrion flock diseased sheep
nine-men's-morris outdoor game
 (like draughts)

distemperature disorder
old Hiems winter
childing pregnant, fruitful
mazèd amazed, confused (a word
 used frequently in the play)
progeny offspring
dissension disagreement

TITANIA These are the forgeries of jealousy:
And never since the middle summer's spring
Met we on hill, in dale, forest, or mead,
By pavèd fountain or by rushy brook,
Or in the beachèd margent of the sea   85
To dance our ringlets to the whistling wind,
But with thy brawls thou hast disturbed our sport.
Therefore the winds, piping to us in vain,
As in revenge have sucked up from the sea
Contagious fogs; which, falling in the land,   90
Hath every pelting river made so proud
That they have overborne their continents.
The ox hath therefore stretched his yoke in vain,
The ploughman lost his sweat, and the green corn
Hath rotted ere his youth attained a beard.   95
The fold stands empty in the drownèd field,
And crows are fatted with the murrion flock;
The nine-men's-morris is filled up with mud,
And the quaint mazes in the wanton green
For lack of tread are undistinguishable.   100
The human mortals want their winter cheer;
No night is now with hymn or carol blessed.
Therefore the moon, the governess of floods,
Pale in her anger, washes all the air,
That rheumatic diseases do abound;   105
And thorough this distemperature we see
The seasons alter; hoary-headed frosts
Fall in the fresh lap of the crimson rose,
And on old Hiems' thin and icy crown
An odorous chaplet of sweet summer buds   110
Is, as in mockery, set. The spring, the summer,
The childing autumn, angry winter change
Their wonted liveries, and the mazèd world
By their increase now knows not which is which.
And this same progeny of evils comes   115
From our debate, from our dissension.
We are their parents and original.

Oberon asks Titania to give up her 'changeling boy', the subject of the quarrel. She explains why she is going to keep him, and Oberon promises to be revenged.

1 Titania refuses a male command (in pairs)

Look carefully at Titania's reasons for keeping the boy (lines 123–37). Once again, a male is trying to dominate a female. Talk together about where your sympathies lie.

2 To cut or not to cut? (in pairs)

Shakespeare's plays are often cut for performance (that is, shortened by leaving some lines or speeches out). Take parts and read lines 118–47 aloud, and then speak them again leaving out lines 123–37. To find the difference that cutting these lines makes, list what is gained against what is lost. Then take an editorial decision about what to do in your production of this episode.

3 Hippolyta, Theseus, Oberon and Titania (in groups of four)

a Each person takes one role. In role, discuss your situation, your relationships and your problems. Question each other on what you are thinking and feeling. Try to find some common ground. You might suggest solutions to each other's problems.

b Take a part and start with a statement of fact. Then disclose your thoughts and feelings. For example, begin with 'My name is Theseus, I am duke of Athens. In four days I will marry Hippolyta.' This will make a good speaking and listening assignment.

c Shakespeare is probably presenting the fairy world as mirroring relationships in the mortal world. Identify the thematic and linguistic echoes of the lovers, and decide if you think the fairies are parodying the human world here.

---

henchman page
votress member of religious order, worshipper
embarkèd traders traders who had set sail

wanton mischievous, immoral
swimming gait gliding movement
Perchance maybe
spare avoid
chide downright argue

OBERON Do you amend it, then: it lies in you.
    Why should Titania cross her Oberon?
    I do but beg a little changeling boy   120
    To be my henchman.
TITANIA   Set your heart at rest.
    The fairy land buys not the child of me.
    His mother was a votress of my order,
    And in the spicèd Indian air by night
    Full often hath she gossiped by my side,   125
    And sat with me on Neptune's yellow sands
    Marking th'embarkèd traders on the flood,
    When we have laughed to see the sails conceive
    And grow big-bellied with the wanton wind;
    Which she, with pretty and with swimming gait 130
    Following (her womb then rich with my young squire),
    Would imitate, and sail upon the land
    To fetch me trifles, and return again
    As from a voyage, rich with merchandise.
    But she, being mortal, of that boy did die,   135
    And for her sake do I rear up her boy;
    And for her sake I will not part with him.
OBERON How long within this wood intend you stay?
TITANIA Perchance till after Theseus' wedding day.
    If you will patiently dance in our round,   140
    And see our moonlight revels, go with us:
    If not, shun me, and I will spare your haunts.
OBERON Give me that boy, and I will go with thee.
TITANIA Not for thy fairy kingdom! Fairies, away.
    We shall chide downright if I longer stay.   145
           Exeunt [Titania and her train]
OBERON Well, go thy way. Thou shalt not from this grove
    Till I torment thee for this injury.

Oberon tells Puck to fetch him 'love-in-idleness' (a flower touched by Cupid's arrow). When the juice of the flower is put on the eyelids of the sleeping, it makes them fall in love with whatever they first see when they awake.

1 Fit actions and reactions to the words (in pairs)

The director has asked you to choreograph a pacey and action-packed presentation of Oberon's speech. Work out a series of actions for Oberon and reactions for Puck. Present your action-filled performance.

Since when
dulcet soothing, quiet
spheres orbits
vestal virgin (Queen Elizabeth I?)
Cupid's fiery shaft Cupid's arrow which was supposed to make the person hit fall in love

imperial votress (Queen Elizabeth I?)
bolt arrow
leviathan whale

My gentle Puck, come hither. Thou rememberest
Since once I sat upon a promontory,
And heard a mermaid on a dolphin's back   150
Uttering such dulcet and harmonious breath
That the rude sea grew civil at her song,
And certain stars shot madly from their spheres
To hear the sea-maid's music?

PUCK   I remember.

OBERON That very time I saw (but thou couldst not)   155
Flying between the cold moon and the earth
Cupid all armed: a certain aim he took
At a fair vestal thronèd by the west,
And loosed his loveshaft smartly from his bow
As it should pierce a hundred thousand hearts;   160
But I might see young Cupid's fiery shaft
Quenched in the chaste beams of the watery moon;
And the imperial votress passèd on
In maiden meditation, fancy-free.
Yet marked I where the bolt of Cupid fell: 165
It fell upon a little western flower,
Before, milk-white; now purple with love's wound:
And maidens call it 'love-in-idleness'.
Fetch me that flower, the herb I showed thee once;
The juice of it on sleeping eyelids laid   170
Will make or man or woman madly dote
Upon the next live creature that it sees.
Fetch me this herb, and be thou here again
Ere the leviathan can swim a league.

PUCK I'll put a girdle round about the earth   175
In forty minutes!   [*Exit*]

Oberon plans to use the flower's juice on Titania, then makes himself invisible as Demetrius and Helena enter, arguing. He is looking for Hermia, and Helena has followed him.

1 Oberon's revenge – your view (in pairs)

Read aloud Oberon's lines 176–85, and then consider whether he is fair in doing this. You are probably forming an opinion of Oberon. If he were human, what would you think of him?

2 The fairy, the audience, the mortal world (in groups of four)

Oberon is on the stage alone at first. His soliloquy tells of his intended revenge. Speculate on the kind of relationship Shakespeare envisaged him having with the audience here. In particular, discuss whether he might speak some or all of his lines direct to the audience. Oberon is, however, invisible to the mortals. This – and what has gone before – suggests the extent of his powers. As you read on, you will find the fairy and the mortal worlds collide hilariously.

3 The lovers' argument (in pairs)

a Lines 188–213 are a good example of Shakespeare's fondness for wordplay. Read the lines aloud and identify some of the different kinds of wordplay. Read them again, emphasising the wordplay. Discuss whether you would wish to use it to make this a funny or a cruel episode.

b Read through the argument again, thinking about what the characters are feeling. Like Titania and Oberon, they are upset and angry. What do you think about the image that Helena uses of being Demetrius's dog? Try reading it to emphasise these feelings.

c Now act out the argument, perhaps in different ways, stressing the feelings, or the silliness of it all.

---

wood (line 192) mad, insane while he is in a real wood. Elizabethans were fond of wordplay and puns, as this episode shows.

adamant hard stone, diamond
Leave you give up

OBERON   Having once this juice
           I'll watch Titania when she is asleep,
           And drop the liquor of it in her eyes:
           The next thing then she, waking, looks upon –
           Be it on lion, bear, or wolf, or bull,   180
           On meddling monkey, or on busy ape –
           She shall pursue it with the soul of love.
           And ere I take this charm from off her sight
           (As I can take it with another herb)
           I'll make her render up her page to me.   185
           But who comes here? I am invisible,
           And I will overhear their conference.

           Enter DEMETRIUS, HELENA *following him.*

DEMETRIUS I love thee not, therefore pursue me not.
           Where is Lysander, and fair Hermia?
           The one I'll slay, the other slayeth me.   190
           Thou told'st me they were stol'n unto this wood,
           And here am I, and wood within this wood
           Because I cannot meet my Hermia.
           Hence, get thee gone, and follow me no more.
HELENA You draw me, you hard-hearted adamant!   195
           But yet you draw not iron, for my heart
           Is true as steel. Leave you your power to draw,
           And I shall have no power to follow you.
DEMETRIUS Do I entice you? Do I speak you fair?
           Or rather do I not in plainest truth   200
           Tell you I do not, nor I cannot love you?
HELENA And even for that do I love you the more.
           I am your spaniel; and, Demetrius,
           The more you beat me I will fawn on you.
           Use me but as your spaniel: spurn me, strike me,   205
           Neglect me, lose me; only give me leave,
           Unworthy as I am, to follow you.
           What worser place can I beg in your love
           (And yet a place of high respect with me)
           Than to be usèd as you use your dog?   210
DEMETRIUS Tempt not too much the hatred of my spirit;
           For I am sick when I do look on thee.
HELENA And I am sick when I look not on you.

Helena continues to woo Demetrius. He is angry and frustrated at her persistence, and eventually he runs off. She follows him.

1 Women at night (in pairs)

a The physical threat Take turns to speak Demetrius's lines 214–19 as menacingly as you can, and think carefully about the implications of his threat. Women often feel more vulnerable at night, especially in places like a wood. The problem of women's safety at night was as real in Shakespeare's day as today. Speaking the lines menacingly adds a contemporary relevance to the play. What tone do you think the actor should use?

b The moral threat However, Shakespeare may not have been considering Helena's physical safety as much as the threat to her reputation and respectability. Either way, it adds an unpleasantly hard edge to what is surely a light-hearted play. What other 'hard edges' have you noticed so far in the play?

2 Demetrius – what's he like?

Demetrius is a problem character. He appears to be unpleasant and aggressive in this scene. How would you play him? Write down some ideas and consider audience reaction. Also note any parallels between him, Theseus, Oberon and Egeus.

3 Write a couplet for Demetrius

Helena's final couplet (the two rhyming lines 243–4) sums up her feelings. Write a couplet for Demetrius to say to Helena just before he leaves that sums up *his* feelings.

impeach call into question	**hind** deer	
desert lonely, deserted	**bootless** useless	
brakes undergrowth, thicket	**stay** endure	
griffin beast, half-eagle and half-lion	**upon** by means of	

DEMETRIUS You do impeach your modesty too much,
    To leave the city and commit yourself 215
    Into the hands of one that loves you not;
    To trust the opportunity of night,
    And the ill counsel of a desert place,
    With the rich worth of your virginity.
HELENA Your virtue is my privilege: for that 220
    It is not night when I do see your face,
    Therefore I think I am not in the night;
    Nor doth this wood lack worlds of company,
    For you, in my respect, are all the world.
    Then how can it be said I am alone 225
    When all the world is here to look on me?
DEMETRIUS I'll run from thee and hide me in the brakes,
    And leave thee to the mercy of wild beasts.
HELENA The wildest hath not such a heart as you.
    Run when you will: the story shall be changed; 230
    Apollo flies, and Daphne holds the chase,
    The dove pursues the griffin, the mild hind
    Makes speed to catch the tiger – bootless speed,
    When cowardice pursues, and valour flies!
DEMETRIUS I will not stay thy questions. Let me go; 235
    Or if thou follow me, do not believe
    But I shall do thee mischief in the wood.
HELENA Ay, in the temple, in the town, the field,
    You do me mischief. Fie, Demetrius,
    Your wrongs do set a scandal on my sex! 240
    We cannot fight for love, as men may do;
    We should be wooed, and were not made to woo.
                          [*Exit Demetrius*]

    I'll follow thee, and make a heaven of hell,
    To die upon the hand I love so well. *Exit*

Oberon vows to help Helena. Puck returns with the flower. Oberon will use it on Titania when she is asleep. He tells Puck to drop the juice of it in Demetrius's eyes when Helena is near.

1 Out of this world

What impression of the fairies do you gain from the photograph of Puck and Oberon above? How do you think this Oberon would speak lines 248–67? Try out your version of the lines, then speak them in the style of the Oberon shown in the pictures on page vi, x (bottom) and xii (top) in the colour section, and on pages 30, 92 and 152. Afterwards, make brief notes on how the physical appearance of each Oberon affected your style of speaking.

nymph beautiful woodland creature   **Weed** cloth
sometime of during

OBERON Fare thee well, nymph. Ere he do leave this grove   245
Thou shalt fly him, and he shall seek thy love.

Enter Puck.

Hast thou the flower there? Welcome, wanderer.
PUCK Ay, there it is.
OBERON   I pray thee give it me.
I know a bank where the wild thyme blows,
Where oxlips and the nodding violet grows,   250
Quite overcanopied with luscious woodbine,
With sweet musk-roses, and with eglantine:
There sleeps Titania sometime of the night,
Lulled in these flowers with dances and delight;
And there the snake throws her enamelled skin,   255
Weed wide enough to wrap a fairy in;
And with the juice of this I'll streak her eyes,
And make her full of hateful fantasies.
Take thou some of it, and seek through this grove:
A sweet Athenian lady is in love   260
With a disdainful youth; anoint his eyes,
But do it when the next thing he espies
May be the lady. Thou shalt know the man
By the Athenian garments he hath on.
Effect it with some care, that he may prove   265
More fond on her than she upon her love.
And look thou meet me ere the first cock crow.
PUCK Fear not, my lord; your servant shall do so.

Exeunt

Titania orders the fairies to sing her to sleep – and they sing a lullaby. A single fairy is left to guard the sleeping Titania.

This is how the Chichester Festival Theatre presented Titania and the fairies in 2004. Think about the variety of ways in which you could stage them (body position, facial expression and so on). Pick a fairy moment from the play and create a variety of tableaux. Photograph them, if possible. If you use a digital camera you can photo-edit the images for surreal or superhuman effects. If you have the resources, experiment with make-up and costumes.

1 Make your own music

Take four lines from the lullaby and compose a melody line for it.

a roundel a dance in a circle	**offices** jobs
cankers caterpillars	**double tongue** forked tongue
reremice bats	**Philomel** nightingale

Act 2 Scene 2
The wood

Enter TITANIA, Queen of Fairies, with her train.

TITANIA Come, now a roundel and a fairy song,
　　　　Then for the third part of a minute, hence –
　　　　Some to kill cankers in the musk-rose buds,
　　　　Some war with reremice for their leathern wings
　　　　To make my small elves coats, and some keep back   5
　　　　The clamorous owl that nightly hoots and wonders
　　　　At our quaint spirits. Sing me now asleep;
　　　　Then to your offices, and let me rest.
　　　　　　　　　　　　Fairies sing.
[FIRST FAIRY] You spotted snakes with double tongue,
　　　　　　Thorny hedgehogs, be not seen.   10
　　　　　　Newts and blindworms, do no wrong,
　　　　　　Come not near our Fairy Queen.
[CHORUS]　　Philomel with melody
　　　　　　Sing in our sweet lullaby,
　　　　　　Lulla, lulla, lullaby; lulla, lulla, lullaby.   15
　　　　　　　　Never harm
　　　　　　　　Nor spell nor charm
　　　　　　Come our lovely lady nigh.
　　　　　　So good night, with lullaby.
FIRST FAIRY Weaving spiders, come not here;   20
　　　　　　Hence, you longlegged spinners, hence!
　　　　　　Beetles black approach not near;
　　　　　　Worm nor snail, do no offence.
[CHORUS]　　Philomel with melody
　　　　　　Sing in our sweet lullaby,   25
　　　　　　Lulla, lulla, lullaby; lulla, lulla, lullaby.
　　　　　　　　Never harm
　　　　　　　　Nor spell nor charm
　　　　　　Come our lovely lady nigh.
　　　　　　So good night, with lullaby.   30
　　　　　　　　　　Titania sleeps.
SECOND FAIRY
　　　　　　Hence, away! Now all is well;
　　　　　　One aloof stand sentinel!
　　　　　　　　　　　　[Exeunt Fairies]

Oberon puts the flower's juice on Titania's eyes with a charm that she will wake 'when some vile thing is near!' and fall in love with it. Lysander and Hermia enter, lost. She rejects his advances and they prepare to sleep.

1 Contrasting kinds of love (in groups of three)

Take parts and read lines 33–67. Afterwards, talk together about the different kinds of love shown here (Oberon's, Lysander's and Hermia's).

2 Irony – what Lysander doesn't know

Line 67 is ironic (because Lysander's love alters in a few minutes, thanks to Puck putting the flower's juice on his eyes instead of Demetrius's). As you read on, look out for other examples of irony in what people say or do. See also page 156.

---

languish droop, pine
ounce lynx
Pard leopard

tarry wait
troth truth
much beshrew a curse upon

Enter OBERON; [*he squeezes the juice on Titania's eyes*].

OBERON What thou seest when thou dost wake,
  Do it for thy true love take;
  Love and languish for his sake.   35
  Be it ounce or cat or bear,
  Pard, or boar with bristled hair
  In thy eye that shall appear
  When thou wak'st, it is thy dear.
  Wake when some vile thing is near!   [*Exit*]   40

    Enter LYSANDER *and* HERMIA.

LYSANDER Fair love, you faint with wandering in the wood,
  And, to speak truth, I have forgot our way.
  We'll rest us, Hermia, if you think it good,
  And tarry for the comfort of the day.
HERMIA Be it so, Lysander; find you out a bed,   45
  For I upon this bank will rest my head.
LYSANDER One turf shall serve as pillow for us both;
  One heart, one bed, two bosoms, and one troth.
HERMIA Nay, good Lysander, for my sake, my dear,
  Lie further off yet; do not lie so near.   50
LYSANDER O take the sense, sweet, of my innocence!
  Love takes the meaning in love's conference;
  I mean that my heart unto yours is knit,
  So that but one heart we can make of it:
  Two bosoms interchainèd with an oath,   55
  So then two bosoms and a single troth.
  Then by your side no bed-room me deny,
  For lying so, Hermia, I do not lie.
HERMIA Lysander riddles very prettily.
  Now much beshrew my manners and my pride   60
  If Hermia meant to say Lysander lied.
  But, gentle friend, for love and courtesy
  Lie further off, in human modesty;
  Such separation as may well be said
  Becomes a virtuous bachelor and a maid,   65
  So far be distant, and good night, sweet friend;
  Thy love ne'er alter till thy sweet life end!

Hermia and Lysander sleep, and Puck mistakenly puts the juice in Lysander's eyes. Demetrius enters, chased still by Helena. He quickly leaves again, on his own, and goes into the woods.

---

1 The lovers think of the past – and future

Write down the thoughts and feelings of Hermia and Lysander as they drift off to sleep. What are they individually thinking about: what has happened so far, the difference of opinion they have just had, or their plans and hopes for the future? Try writing in rhyming couplets as Shakespeare does here.

2 The fairy touch (in pairs)

In this scene, the fairy world – through Puck – directly manipulates the feelings of a mortal. Every new production of the play spends much time in rehearsal working out how to present this, because the consequences of such influence could be disturbing. How would you want Puck to speak and behave here?

To help you decide, take roles, one person as Puck, the other as director. Act out Puck's speech, focusing on his attitude to the mortal whose life he is changing. Swap roles and create different attitudes displayed by Puck, mischievous, sinister and so on.

3 Emphasise the rhymes? (in pairs)

There are over seven hundred rhyming lines in the play. Actors always talk together about whether the rhymes should be emphasised. Some argue they should; others claim that the syntax is more important, so that the meaning is clearly conveyed to the audience. They say that the lines should 'run on' where appropriate, to bring out the meaning.

Explore by trying the different approaches with the lines opposite (in Shakespeare's day, 'gone' rhymed with 'none').

---

approve put to the proof
Weeds clothes
Churl heartless rogue

owe possess
darkling sad, downcast

LYSANDER Amen, amen, to that fair prayer say I,
And then end life when I end loyalty!
Here is my bed; sleep give thee all his rest.   70
HERMIA With half that wish the wisher's eyes be pressed.
They sleep.

Enter PUCK.

PUCK   Through the forest have I gone,
              But Athenian found I none
              On whose eyes I might approve
              This flower's force in stirring love.   75
              Night and silence – Who is here?
              Weeds of Athens he doth wear:
              This is he my master said
              Despisèd the Athenian maid;
              And here the maiden, sleeping sound   80
              On the dank and dirty ground.
              Pretty soul, she durst not lie
              Near this lack-love, this kill-courtesy.
              Churl, upon thy eyes I throw
              All the power this charm doth owe.   85
              [*He squeezes the juice on Lysander's eyes.*]
              When thou wak'st let love forbid
              Sleep his seat on thy eyelid.
              So, awake when I am gone;
              For I must now to Oberon.   *Exit*

Enter DEMETRIUS *and* HELENA, *running.*

HELENA Stay, though thou kill me, sweet Demetrius!   90
DEMETRIUS I charge thee, hence, and do not haunt me thus.
HELENA O wilt thou darkling leave me? Do not so!
DEMETRIUS Stay, on thy peril; I alone will go.   *Exit*

Helena stops to rest and sees Lysander. He wakes up, and immediately falls in love with Helena because of the flower's magic.

1 Shall I compare me to a bear?

Read through Helena's speech about her own appearance (lines 94–108). Why might she feel this way about herself?

2 Lysander – or 'raw passion'? (in pairs)

a An actor who played Lysander said this: 'Lysander gets taken over when he's under the influence of magic; that's where character tends to disappear. It brings out all this raw passion.' Think about what he means by 'character tends to disappear', and try various ways of presenting a transformed Lysander. Share ideas with other groups, and discuss the implications for performance.

b 'And run through fire I will for thy sweet sake!' The audience knows that Lysander's 'love' is just magic, but for Helena the Athenian world of conventions and normality must seem far away. Line 109 is often played as farce. Work out how you would perform it to bring out what Helena thinks of Lysander's sudden transformation.

3 The dance of lovers – who loves whom? (II)

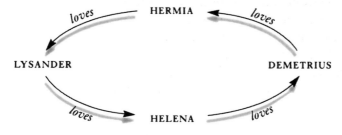

fond foolish
dissembling concealing, disguising
glass mirror
sphery eyne star-like eyes

Transparent honest, open
ripe mature
touching reaching

HELENA O, I am out of breath in this fond chase!
        The more my prayer, the lesser is my grace.   95
        Happy is Hermia, wheresoe'er she lies,
        For she hath blessèd and attractive eyes.
        How came her eyes so bright? Not with salt tears –
        If so, my eyes are oftener washed than hers.
        No, no, I am as ugly as a bear,   100
        For beasts that meet me run away for fear.
        Therefore no marvel though Demetrius
        Do as a monster fly my presence thus.
        What wicked and dissembling glass of mine
        Made me compare with Hermia's sphery eyne?   105
        But who is here? – Lysander, on the ground?
        Dead, or asleep? I see no blood, no wound.
        Lysander, if you live, good sir, awake!
LYSANDER [*Waking.*]
        And run through fire I will for thy sweet sake!
        Transparent Helena, nature shows art   110
        That through thy bosom makes me see thy heart.
        Where is Demetrius? O, how fit a word
        Is that vile name to perish on my sword!
HELENA Do not say so, Lysander, say not so.
        What though he love your Hermia? Lord, what though?   115
        Yet Hermia still loves you; then be content.
LYSANDER Content with Hermia? No; I do repent
        The tedious minutes I with her have spent.
        Not Hermia, but Helena I love.
        Who will not change a raven for a dove?   120
        The will of man is by his reason swayed,
        And reason says you are the worthier maid.
        Things growing are not ripe until their season;
        So I, being young, till now ripe not to reason.
        And touching now the point of human skill,   125
        Reason becomes the marshal to my will.
        And leads me to your eyes, where I o'erlook
        Love's stories written in love's richest book.

Helena thinks Lysander is making fun of her, and leaves. He follows, leaving Hermia behind, still asleep. Hermia wakes from a nightmare, realises she is alone, and goes to find Lysander.

---

1 Three moods, three 'dreams' (in groups of three)

a There are three characters, three moods and three different 'dreams' of what is happening here. None of the three characters really understands what is going on. Each person chooses a character, reads their speech aloud, and describes the character's mood and 'dream' of what is happening.

b Concentrate on Hermia's dream. Talk together about what it might mean. Share your views on whether you agree that dreams sometimes highlight subconscious fears or preoccupations. Give actual examples if you can.

2 Male speech? Female speech? (in groups of three)

Compare the two women's speeches opposite, and see if there are any similarities. Then contrast them with Lysander's. If you find differences between the male and female speeches, share them with the class and discuss the implications.

3 Disturbing images

a Remind yourselves of the 'dance' of the lovers on page 50 – things couldn't get worse. List as many negative/upsetting images as you can in lines 94–162. When you have compiled your list, write a paragraph saying how the images suggest that the midsummer night's dream is becoming a nightmare.

b Hermia entered the wood with high hopes. Compare the world she finds herself in now (the wood, the night, the magic) with the one she left behind. Write several sentences giving your view about whether her situation now is as bad as it was at the beginning of the play.

---

keen sharp		**surfeit** surplus	
flout mock		**heresies** false religious beliefs	
good sooth in truth, indeed		**swoon** faint	
perforce of necessity		**nigh** near	

HELENA Wherefore was I to this keen mockery born?
When at your hands did I deserve this scorn?   130
Is't not enough, is't not enough, young man,
That I did never, no, nor never can
Deserve a sweet look from Demetrius' eye
But you must flout my insufficiency?
Good troth, you do me wrong, good sooth, you do,   135
In such disdainful manner me to woo!
But fare you well: perforce I must confess
I thought you lord of more true gentleness.
O, that a lady of one man refused
Should of another therefore be abused!   *Exit*   140

LYSANDER She sees not Hermia. Hermia, sleep thou there,
And never mayst thou come Lysander near.
For, as a surfeit of the sweetest things
The deepest loathing to the stomach brings,
Or as the heresies that men do leave   145
Are hated most of those they did deceive,
So thou, my surfeit and my heresy,
Of all be hated, but the most of me!
And, all my powers, address your love and might
To honour Helen, and to be her knight.   *Exit*   150

HERMIA [*Waking.*]
Help me, Lysander, help me! Do thy best
To pluck this crawling serpent from my breast!
Ay me, for pity! What a dream was here!
Lysander, look how I do quake with fear –
Methought a serpent ate my heart away,   155
And you sat smiling at his cruel prey.
Lysander! What, removed? Lysander, lord!
What, out of hearing? Gone? No sound, no word?
Alack, where are you? Speak and if you hear.
Speak, of all loves! I swoon almost with fear.   160
No? Then I well perceive you are not nigh.
Either death or you I'll find immediately.   *Exit*

Looking back at Act 2
Activities for groups or individuals

What impression of the fairy world do you get from this photograph? Write a paragraph giving your response.

1 Design a set for all scenes

Modern productions flow swiftly from scene to scene. There are no long scene-shifting delays. The play moves between the court, the home of one of the Mechanicals, and the wood. Step into role as designer. Sketch and write details of a simple set that persuades the audience the scene has shifted.

2 Love and magic: ancient and modern

In Scene 1, lines 155–74, Oberon tells of the flower whose juice on a sleeper's eyelids makes them 'madly dote' on the first person they see when they wake. The idea of love potions is ancient, but even today the connection is often made between love and magic. Use your experience of the play so far to write an essay on the subject 'Love and magic in *Dream*, and today's world'.

3 Who's who?

Many people get confused between the lovers in *A Midsummer Night's Dream*, particularly when the lovers begin to swap and change who loves whom.

Experiment with ways to remember which lover is which in terms of their distinct characteristics. For example:

Helena is tall.
Hermia is small.
They might be dressed in distinctive colours.

Carry on playing with similar ideas. How might a director help the audience separate Lysander and Demetrius, despite their being of similar age, rank and status?

4 Male dominance

In his two speeches on page 43, Oberon shows his power over the lives of both mortals and fairies. That reinforces the sense that male characters dominate the play (Theseus in Athens, Oberon in the wood). Perhaps this is Shakespeare reflecting the realities and prejudices of his time. Or perhaps it reflects the fact that they have positions of great power (duke, king). Discuss whether this male domination influences your responses to the characters or to the play. Give examples.

5 Act 2 – a fast-forward version

Act 2 is filled with moments of high drama: the quarrel between Oberon and Titania, Demetrius rejecting Helena and abandoning her, Oberon squeezing the juice into Titania's eyes, Puck mistakenly doing the same to Lysander's with comical results and Helena's bewilderment, Hermia's waking anguish. Use these moments (and others) to create a three-minute version of Act 2.

In the wood near the sleeping Titania, the Mechanicals begin their rehearsal with Bottom suggesting changes in the play to make it less frightening.

Choose a quotation from the script opposite as an appropriate caption for this photograph of the Mechanicals.

Pat on the dot, on time	**By'r lakin** By Our Lady (an
brake thicket	exclamation)
tiring-house dressing room	**parlous** perilous
bully (adjective that implies respect	
and admiration)	

Act 3 Scene 1
The wood

Enter the Clowns [, BOTTOM, QUINCE, SNOUT, STARVELING, SNUG and FLUTE. TITANIA remains on stage, asleep].

BOTTOM Are we all met?

QUINCE Pat, pat; and here's a marvellous convenient place for our rehearsal. This green plot shall be our stage, this hawthorn brake our tiring-house, and we will do it in action as we will do it before the Duke. 5

BOTTOM Peter Quince!

QUINCE What sayest thou, bully Bottom?

BOTTOM There are things in this comedy of Pyramus and Thisbe that will never please. First, Pyramus must draw a sword to kill himself, which the ladies cannot abide. How answer you that? 10

SNOUT By'r lakin, a parlous fear!

STARVELING I believe we must leave the killing out, when all is done.

BOTTOM Not a whit; I have a device to make all well. Write me a prologue, and let the prologue seem to say we will do no harm with our swords, and that Pyramus is not killed indeed; and for the more 15 better assurance, tell them that I, Pyramus, am not Pyramus, but Bottom the weaver: this will put them out of fear.

QUINCE Well, we will have such a prologue; and it shall be written in eight and six.

BOTTOM No, make it two more: let it be written in eight and eight. 20

SNOUT Will not the ladies be afeard of the lion?

STARVELING I fear it, I promise you.

BOTTOM Masters, you ought to consider with yourself, to bring in (God shield us!) a lion among ladies is a most dreadful thing; for there is not a more fearful wildfowl than your lion living; and we ought 25 to look to't.

SNOUT Therefore another prologue must tell he is not a lion.

BOTTOM Nay, you must name his name, and half his face must be seen through the lion's neck, and he himself must speak through, saying thus, or to the same defect: 'Ladies', or 'Fair ladies, I would wish 30 you', or 'I would request you', or 'I would entreat you, not to fear, not to tremble: my life for yours. If you think I come hither as a lion, it were pity of my life. No, I am no such thing; I am a man,

The Mechanicals discuss how to show moonlight and the wall in the play, and decide they must have an actor represent each.

1 Act it out! (in groups of seven)

The first half of this scene (lines 1–98) shows the Mechanicals preparing to rehearse, and Puck's mischievous interference. To gain a first impression of what happens, take parts as the Mechanicals and Puck, and read lines 1–98. Don't pause over anything you don't understand – just enjoy the comedy. When you have completed your read-through, work on some of the activities provided.

2 Bottom – always full of ideas (in groups of six)

Peter Quince has written the play, but in this scene the audience hears only a tiny fraction of it. You will have to wait until Act 5 to discover just what script the Mechanicals intend to act. But Bottom, as usual, is full of suggestions and ideas.

a One person steps into role as Bottom and speaks all that he says in lines 1–55. The others play the other Mechanicals. You will find that Bottom does most of the talking. As you speak Bottom's lines, add the sort of gestures and actions you think he would make. Take turns to play Bottom, so that everyone gets a chance to experience his sheer enthusiasm.

b Each person in role as one of the Mechanicals explains what their character thinks of Bottom from what he says and does in lines 1–55. Include what Bottom thinks of himself. Then talk together about what you personally think about Bottom and compare your views with what the Mechanicals think of their friend.

c Compile a list of all the suggestions that Bottom makes. Alongside each, write whether or not you think it is sensible.

---

almanac calendar which often includes astronomical information
casement hinged window

loam clay for brick making
rough-cast rough coating for a wall

as other men are' – and there indeed let him name his name, and
tell them plainly he is Snug the joiner.   35

QUINCE Well, it shall be so. But there is two hard things: that is, to
bring the moonlight into a chamber; for, you know, Pyramus and
Thisbe meet by moonlight.

SNUG Doth the moon shine that night we play our play?

BOTTOM A calendar, a calendar! Look in the almanac – find out   40
moonshine, find out moonshine!

QUINCE Yes, it doth shine that night.

BOTTOM Why, then may you leave a casement of the great chamber
window, where we play, open, and the moon may shine in at the
casement.   45

QUINCE Ay; or else one must come in with a bush of thorns and a
lantern, and say he comes to disfigure, or to present the person of
Moonshine. Then there is another thing: we must have a wall in
the great chamber; for Pyramus and Thisbe, says the story, did talk
through the chink of a wall.   50

SNOUT You can never bring in a wall. What say you, Bottom?

BOTTOM Some man or other must present Wall; and let him have some
plaster, or some loam, or some rough-cast about him to signify Wall;
or let him hold his fingers thus, and through that cranny shall
Pyramus and Thisbe whisper.   55

QUINCE If that may be, then all is well. Come, sit down every mother's
son, and rehearse your parts. Pyramus, you begin. When you have
spoken your speech, enter into that brake, and so everyone
according to his cue.

Puck enters, and watches as the Mechanicals begin to rehearse, going off with
Bottom when he goes off stage. After getting his lines muddled, Flute gives
Bottom his cue to reappear.

---

1 A rehearsal – and bad acting (in groups of three)

Not only is there a play within *A Midsummer Night's Dream* (in Act 5),
there are even rehearsals. Many people think that Shakespeare was
mocking groups of actors who travelled around England in the early
years of Queen Elizabeth's reign. Others think he was poking fun
at amateur dramatics because he was in one of the first professional
theatre companies in England.

Whatever the reason, Shakespeare knew how to present bad acting.
He does that in the lines opposite. First, talk together about the
complications of acting characters who are attempting to act well,
but failing. Then take parts as Quince, Bottom and Flute and speak
lines 64–84 to show how the timing of the lines helps to bring out
the Mechanicals' bad acting.

2 Puck, invisible, transforms Bottom (in groups of seven)

Puck is 'invisible' (the Mechanicals can't see him, but the audience
can). When you turn the page you will discover that he has placed an
ass's head on Bottom. That transformation has a frightening effect
on the other Mechanicals.

a Take parts as the Mechanicals and Puck and act out lines
 60–106. The farce of the rehearsal turns into the farce of Bottom
 being an ass, and it offers lots of opportunities for knockabout
 comedy, even for those who do not speak. If you can, video the
 scene, using close-ups and cuts, or perform it directly to the rest
 of the class.

b It will help your performance if you look at some of the ways in
 which Bottom has been transformed in different productions.
 See the pictures in the colour section, and on pages 62, 64, 66
 and 156.

---

hempen homespuns the
 Mechanicals are dressed in rough,
 homemade clothes

lilywhite of hue pale coloured
brisky juvenal lively young man
eke also

Enter PUCK.

PUCK   What hempen homespuns have we swaggering here   60
   So near the cradle of the Fairy Queen?
   What, a play toward? I'll be an auditor,
   An actor too perhaps, if I see cause.
QUINCE   Speak, Pyramus! Thisbe, stand forth!
BOTTOM   (*as Pyramus*)
   Thisbe, the flowers of odious savours sweet –   65
QUINCE   Odours – 'odorous'!
BOTTOM   (*as Pyramus*)   . . .odours savours sweet.
   So hath thy breath, my dearest Thisbe dear.
   But hark, a voice! Stay thou but here awhile,
   And by and by I will to thee appear.   *Exit* 70
PUCK   A stranger Pyramus than e'er played here.   [*Exit*]
FLUTE   Must I speak now?
QUINCE   Ay, marry must you; for you must understand he goes but to
  see a noise that he heard, and is to come again.
FLUTE   (*as Thisbe*)
   Most radiant Pyramus, most lilywhite of hue,   75
    Of colour like the red rose on triumphant briar,
   Most brisky juvenal, and eke most lovely Jew,
    As true as truest horse that yet would never tire,
   I'll meet thee, Pyramus, at Ninny's tomb –
QUINCE   'Ninus' tomb', man! – Why, you must not speak that yet; that   80
  you answer to Pyramus. You speak all your part at once, cues and
  all. Pyramus, enter – your cue is past. It is 'never tire'.
FLUTE   O –
   (*as Thisbe*)
   As true as truest horse, that yet would never tire.

Bottom re-enters with an ass's head (because of Puck's magic), and all his comrades run away. Bottom thinks that they are teasing him to make him frightened. He sings to show he is unafraid.

'O Bottom, thou art changed. What do I see on thee?' In the Royal National Theatre's 1992 production of *A Midsummer Night's Dream*, Puck's feet became Bottom's ass's ears. Read aloud Puck's lines 88–93 to discover how they add to the Mechanicals' confusion over the strange sight they have just witnessed.

knavery trickery
ousel blackbird
cock male bird

throstle song thrush
little quill quiet song

Enter [Puck], and Bottom with the ass head [on].

BOTTOM (*as Pyramus*)
　　If I were fair, fair Thisbe, I were only thine.　　　　　85
QUINCE O monstrous! O strange! We are haunted! Pray, masters, fly,
　　masters! Help!
Exeunt Quince, Snug, Flute, Snout and Starveling
PUCK　　I'll follow you: I'll lead you about a round,
　　　　Through bog, through bush, through brake, through briar;
　　　　Sometime a horse I'll be, sometime a hound,　　　　90
　　　　　A hog, a headless bear, sometime a fire,
　　　　And neigh, and bark, and grunt, and roar, and burn,
　　　　Like horse, hound, hog, bear, fire at every turn.　　*Exit*
BOTTOM Why do they run away? This is a knavery of them to make
　　me afeard.　　　　　95

Enter Snout.

SNOUT O Bottom, thou art changed. What do I see on thee?
BOTTOM What do you see? You see an ass head of your own, do you?
[Exit Snout]

Enter Quince.

QUINCE Bless thee, Bottom, bless thee! Thou art translated!　*Exit*
BOTTOM I see their knavery. This is to make an ass of me, to fright
　　me, if they could; but I will not stir from this place, do what they　100
　　can. I will walk up and down here, and will sing, that they shall
　　hear I am not afraid.
　　[*Sings.*] The ousel cock so black of hue,
　　　　With orange-tawny bill,
　　　　The throstle with his note so true,　　　　105
　　　　The wren with little quill –

Bottom's song wakes Titania who, under the influence of the potion, instantly falls in love with him. She vows to keep him with her.

1 Transformations – show and speak them (in pairs)

Both characters have been transformed. Bottom's behaviour and speech probably changes (as his head has done) to become more like that of a real ass. Titania, transformed by the love potion, behaves differently from when she confronted Oberon. Experiment with tone, movement and manner for both characters and act out lines 107–36.

2 '. . . reason and love keep little company' (in pairs)

The relationship between reason and love is one of the themes of the play, and Bottom's lines 120–1 stress how far they are apart. *A Midsummer Night's Dream* shows vividly how love makes people act very irrationally. Make a list of the characters who you think are being reasonable, and another list of those who are dominated by their emotions, particularly love.

'What angel wakes me from my flowery bed?' Line 107 is one of Shakespeare's most famous lines, even though it is ironic. Why?

---

set his wit to set his wits against, argue with
give . . . the lie contradict, call a liar
enthrallèd captivated

gleek joke
still doth tend always attends
purge . . . grossness remove human coarseness

TITANIA [*Waking.*] What angel wakes me from my flowery bed?

BOTTOM [*Sings.*]

        The finch, the sparrow, and the lark,
          The plainsong cuckoo grey,
        Whose note full many a man doth mark   110
          And dares not answer nay –

for indeed, who would set his wit to so foolish a bird? Who would give a bird the lie, though he cry 'cuckoo' never so?

TITANIA I pray thee, gentle mortal, sing again;
    Mine ear is much enamoured of thy note.   115
    So is mine eye enthrallèd to thy shape,
    And thy fair virtue's force perforce doth move me
    On the first view to say, to swear, I love thee.

BOTTOM Methinks, mistress, you should have little reason for that. And yet, to say the truth, reason and love keep little company together 120 nowadays; the more the pity that some honest neighbours will not make them friends. Nay, I can gleek upon occasion.

TITANIA Thou art as wise as thou art beautiful.

BOTTOM Not so neither; but if I had wit enough to get out of this wood, I have enough to serve mine own turn.   125

TITANIA Out of this wood do not desire to go:
    Thou shalt remain here, whether thou wilt or no.
    I am a spirit of no common rate;
    The summer still doth tend upon my state,
    And I do love thee. Therefore go with me.   130
    I'll give thee fairies to attend on thee,
    And they shall fetch thee jewels from the deep,
    And sing, while thou on pressèd flowers dost sleep;
    And I will purge thy mortal grossness so
    That thou shalt like an airy spirit go.   135
    Peaseblossom, Cobweb, Moth, and Mustardseed!

Enter four Fairies.

PEASEBLOSSOM Ready.

COBWEB And I.

MOTH And I.

MUSTARDSEED And I.   140

Titania asks her fairies to look after Bottom. He learns their names. Bottom is then led to Titania's bower.

Bottom, lifted by the fairies. Bottom is the only character from the mortal world to see and talk to the fairies. Bottom and Titania have both been transformed. Discuss what sort of relationship they have. Use the photograph above as part of your discussions. Should the audience relate to Titania with humour, sympathy, embarrassment? Or . . .? Suggest how an actress could elicit each response. Put your suggestions into practice by showing how Titania speaks and acts to evoke different responses.

dewberries blackberries
cry . . . mercy beg your pardon

if I cut my finger (cobwebs were used to stop bleeding)

ALL Where shall we go?
TITANIA Be kind and courteous to this gentleman:
        Hop in his walks and gambol in his eyes;
        Feed him with apricocks and dewberries,
        With purple grapes, green figs, and mulberries;   145
        The honey-bags steal from the humble-bees,
        And for night-tapers crop their waxen thighs,
        And light them at the fiery glow-worms' eyes
        To have my love to bed, and to arise;
        And pluck the wings from painted butterflies   150
        To fan the moonbeams from his sleeping eyes.
        Nod to him, elves, and do him courtesies.
PEASEBLOSSOM Hail, mortal!
COBWEB Hail!
MOTH Hail!   155
MUSTARDSEED Hail!
BOTTOM I cry your worships mercy, heartily. I beseech your worship's
    name.
COBWEB Cobweb.
BOTTOM I shall desire you of more acquaintance, good Master Cobweb;   160
    if I cut my finger I shall make bold with you. Your name, honest
    gentleman?
PEASEBLOSSOM Peaseblossom.
BOTTOM I pray you commend me to Mistress Squash, your mother,
    and to Master Peascod, your father. Good Master Peaseblossom,   165
    I shall desire you of more acquaintance, too. – Your name, I
    beseech you, sir?
MUSTARDSEED Mustardseed.
BOTTOM Good Master Mustardseed, I know your patience well. That
    same cowardly, giant-like ox-beef hath devoured many a gentleman   170
    of your house. I promise you, your kindred hath made my eyes
    water ere now. I desire you of more acquaintance, good Master
    Mustardseed.
TITANIA Come, wait upon him. Lead him to my bower.
        The moon methinks looks with a watery eye,   175
      And when she weeps, weeps every little flower,
        Lamenting some enforcèd chastity.
        Tie up my lover's tongue; bring him silently.
                               Exeunt

Oberon wonders who or what Titania now loves. Puck says she loves a 'monster' and explains what he has done to Bottom and the other Mechanicals.

1 Speak it – act it! (in small groups)

Puck tells how he took a hand in the Mechanicals' rehearsal, with hilarious results. Lines 6–34 invite acting out. As one person slowly speaks the lines, the others enact them. Afterwards, discuss why Shakespeare relates as a story what the audience has just seen on stage.

2 Invent some comparisons (in pairs)

Lines 20–3 are an extended metaphor of the Mechanicals and the birds scattering (see p. 164). Compose some extended comparisons yourself, trying to invent ones that capture the Mechanicals' confusion. Write first in prose, and then in rhyming couplets. Read them aloud and discuss which was easier to write.

Is Puck funny, cynical, mischievous, malicious, rude, evil? Choose the word you prefer and find evidence to support your choice.

close secret	**fowler** bird-hunter
consecrated sacred	**russet-pated choughs** grey-headed
patches clowns	jackdaws
rude rough	**apparel** clothes
nole head	**yielders** those running away in fear
mimic actor	

Act 3 Scene 2
The wood

Enter OBERON, *King of Fairies.*

OBERON I wonder if Titania be awaked;
   Then what it was that next came in her eye,
   Which she must dote on, in extremity.

Enter PUCK.

   Here comes my messenger. How now, mad spirit?
   What night-rule now about this haunted grove?   5
PUCK My mistress with a monster is in love.
   Near to her close and consecrated bower,
   While she was in her dull and sleeping hour,
   A crew of patches, rude mechanicals,
   That work for bread upon Athenian stalls,   10
   Were met together to rehearse a play
   Intended for great Theseus' nuptial day.
   The shallowest thick-skin of that barren sort,
   Who Pyramus presented, in their sport
   Forsook his scene and entered in a brake,   15
   When I did him at this advantage take:
   An ass's nole I fixèd on his head.
   Anon his Thisbe must be answerèd,
   And forth my mimic comes. When they him spy –
   As wild geese that the creeping fowler eye,   20
   Or russet-pated choughs, many in sort,
   Rising and cawing at the gun's report,
   Sever themselves and madly sweep the sky –
   So at his sight away his fellows fly,
   And at our stamp here o'er and o'er one falls;   25
   He 'Murder!' cries, and help from Athens calls.
   Their sense thus weak, lost with their fears thus strong,
   Made senseless things begin to do them wrong,
   For briars and thorns at their apparel snatch,
   Some sleeves, some hats; from yielders all things catch.   30

Oberon is pleased to hear that Titania has fallen in love with Bottom. Puck says he has also dealt with the 'Athenian'. Demetrius finds Hermia and tries to court her. She accuses him of having murdered Lysander.

1 The problems of love (in pairs)

Most of Scene 2 will dramatise the growing difficulties of the young lovers. It will show, in Bottom's words, that 'reason and love keep little company'. The first episode, lines 43–87, shows Hermia turning her anger on Demetrius. To gain a first impression of the (one-sided) quarrel, take parts and read the lines. Try to express Hermia's puzzled annoyance and Demetrius's pleading. Afterwards, work on some of the activities.

2 Darkness and confusion (in pairs)

Shakespeare uses language to create emotional atmosphere. Iden-tify words and images in lines 43–81 that best bring out Hermia's and Demetrius's feelings. Read aloud just those words and images. Suggest the mood they create in this episode.

3 Moonlight at noon – impossible

Lysander *did* steal away from Hermia, but her image in lines 53–5 to suggest that is unusual to say the least. It pictures the Earth having a hole bored in it large enough for the moon to pass through, and so annoy the sun (the moon's 'brother') by bringing night at noon with 'th'Antipodes' (those who live on the opposite side of the Earth).

The image is something like certain parts of Titania's speech in Act 2 Scene 1, lines 81–117 because it suggests everything in the nat-ural world is in disorder. Try writing your own image that expresses something that is both impossible and disordered.

---

latched captured, mastered
chide talk angrily
dead pale as death

Venus in Roman mythology, the goddess of love
sphere orbit

I led them on in this distracted fear,
And left sweet Pyramus translated there;
When in that moment, so it came to pass,
Titania waked, and straightway loved an ass.

OBERON   This falls out better than I could devise.   35
But hast thou yet latched the Athenian's eyes
With the love juice, as I did bid thee do?

PUCK   I took him sleeping – that is finished too –
And the Athenian woman by his side,
That when he waked, of force she must be eyed.   40

Enter DEMETRIUS *and* HERMIA.

OBERON   Stand close: this is the same Athenian.

PUCK   This is the woman, but not this the man.

DEMETRIUS   O, why rebuke you him that loves you so?
Lay breath so bitter on your bitter foe.

HERMIA   Now I but chide; but I should use thee worse,   45
For thou, I fear, hast given me cause to curse.
If thou hast slain Lysander in his sleep,
Being o'er shoes in blood, plunge in the deep,
And kill me too.
The sun was not so true unto the day   50
As he to me. Would he have stol'n away
From sleeping Hermia? I'll believe as soon
This whole earth may be bored, and that the moon
May through the centre creep, and so displease
Her brother's noontide with th'Antipodes.   55
It cannot be but thou hast murdered him:
So should a murderer look; so dead, so grim.

DEMETRIUS   So should the murdered look, and so should I,
Pierced through the heart with your stern cruelty;
Yet you, the murderer, look as bright, as clear,   60
As yonder Venus in her glimmering sphere.

HERMIA   What's this to my Lysander? Where is he?
Ah, good Demetrius, wilt thou give him me?

DEMETRIUS   I had rather give his carcass to my hounds.

Hermia storms off, after accusing Demetrius of murder. Demetrius, too tired to follow, goes to sleep. Oberon tells Puck to find Helena in order to correct his mistake.

1 Getting to know the lovers (in pairs)

You have probably already discussed what the lovers were like in Act 1. In this scene you will have plenty more opportunities to learn about them.

a Get to know Hermia and Demetrius further by speaking and listening to just his speeches, and then just her speeches. Discuss the differences between the two characters, and compare your impressions of them here with those earlier in the play. Does either character seem to have changed? In what ways?

b It isn't just different groups in the play, such as the lovers and fairies, that have different views of the world, but also different characters in those groups, such as Hermia and Demetrius. Go through lines 43–81, making notes on what Hermia thinks is going on here, and what Demetrius thinks. Then relate those thoughts to how they are behaving. Suggest similarities to and differences from the encounter between Lysander and Hermia in Act 2 Scene 2.

2 Oberon – different intentions?

Read what Oberon says in his two speeches opposite. Write a paragraph saying what his lines tell you about Oberon and his motives in dealing with the mortals. Then write a further paragraph comparing those motives with his treatment of his wife.

3 Are men fickle? (in pairs)

Puck says 'one man holding troth, / A million fail' (for every man who is true in love, a million are not). Debate whether men are fickle in love, and whether they are more fickle than women.

---

cur coward
worm snake
heaviness weariness
misprision mistake

fancy-sick sick with love
cheer face
Tartar central Asian warrior

HERMIA Out, dog! Out, cur! Thou driv'st me past the bounds 65
    Of maiden's patience. Hast thou slain him then?
    Henceforth be never numbered among men.
    O, once tell true; tell true, even for my sake:
    Durst thou have looked upon him being awake?
    And hast thou killed him sleeping? O, brave touch! 70
    Could not a worm, an adder do so much?
    An adder did it; for with doubler tongue
    Than thine, thou serpent, never adder stung.
DEMETRIUS You spend your passion on a misprised mood.
    I am not guilty of Lysander's blood, 75
    Nor is he dead, for aught that I can tell.
HERMIA I pray thee, tell me then that he is well.
DEMETRIUS And if I could, what should I get therefor?
HERMIA A privilege, never to see me more;
    And from thy hated presence part I so. 80
    See me no more, whether he be dead or no. *Exit*
DEMETRIUS There is no following her in this fierce vein;
    Here therefore for a while I will remain.
    So sorrow's heaviness doth heavier grow
    For debt that bankrupt sleep doth sorrow owe, 85
    Which now in some slight measure it will pay,
    If for his tender here I make some stay.
        [*He*] *lies down* [*and sleeps*].
OBERON What hast thou done? Thou hast mistaken quite,
    And laid the love juice on some true love's sight.
    Of thy misprision must perforce ensue 90
    Some true love turned, and not a false turned true.
PUCK Then fate o'errules, that, one man holding troth,
    A million fail, confounding oath on oath.
OBERON About the wood go swifter than the wind,
    And Helena of Athens look thou find. 95
    All fancy-sick she is and pale of cheer
    With sighs of love, that costs the fresh blood dear.
    By some illusion see thou bring her here;
    I'll charm his eyes against she do appear.
PUCK I go, I go, look how I go! 100
    Swifter than arrow from the Tartar's bow. *Exit*

Oberon puts the magic juice on Demetrius's eyes, and Lysander enters with Helena. He is still trying to convince Helena that he loves her. She thinks he's lying.

1 Puck – a child?

The illustration (from an eighteenth-century book) shows Puck. Today, Puck is usually played by an adult. But folklore about Puck or Robin Goodfellow portrays him as very young. Does he seem childlike?

List the ways in which Puck behaves and thinks like a child. Give quotations and events where he seems pleased at the mayhem, and is rather insensitive to the motives and feelings of the lovers.

Write down how far your findings suggest he is like the illustration.

2 Class direction (whole class)

You need two volunteers – one to play Puck and one to play Oberon. The class directs the actors through lines 88–121. Take all suggestions seriously, try them and evaluate them. Think about:

their relationship   movement   gestures   tone of voice
use of silence   emphasis on particular words   creating dramatic effect

See if the class can come to a united decision about what works best in relation to their vision of the characters in this episode. To work, this needs imagination, confidence and, most importantly, respectful listening skills.

---

apple pupil
fee reward
fond pageant foolish scene

befall prepost'rously turn out absurdly and unnaturally
light as tales fictional as stories

OBERON   *[Squeezing the juice on Demetrius's eyes.]*
Flower of this purple dye,
Hit with Cupid's archery,
Sink in apple of his eye.
When his love he doth espy,   105
Let her shine as gloriously
As the Venus of the sky.
When thou wak'st, if she be by,
Beg of her for remedy.

Enter Puck.

PUCK   Captain of our fairy band,   110
Helena is here at hand,
And the youth mistook by me,
Pleading for a lover's fee.
Shall we their fond pageant see?
Lord, what fools these mortals be!   115

OBERON   Stand aside. The noise they make
Will cause Demetrius to awake.

PUCK   Then will two at once woo one –
That must needs be sport alone;
And those things do best please me   120
That befall prepost'rously.

Enter LYSANDER *and* HELENA.

LYSANDER Why should you think that I should woo in scorn?
Scorn and derision never come in tears.
Look when I vow, I weep; and vows so born,
In their nativity all truth appears.   125
How can these things in me seem scorn to you,
Bearing the badge of faith to prove them true?

HELENA You do advance your cunning more and more.
When truth kills truth, O devilish-holy fray!
These vows are Hermia's. Will you give her o'er?   130
Weigh oath with oath, and you will nothing weigh;
Your vows to her and me, put in two scales,
Will even weigh, and both as light as tales.

LYSANDER I had no judgement when to her I swore.

Demetrius wakes, and tells Helena in very exaggerated language how much he loves her. She thinks that he is part of the plot to mock her.

1 The dance of the lovers – who loves whom? (III)

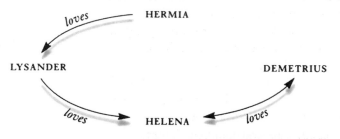

Colour – how important? In the production above, the lovers wore white. A different production (see p. 80) had the lovers in bright primary colours. What effect might the choice of costume colours have on the interpretation of both character and situation? Suggest your own ideas on how colour could be used in the lovers' scenes. The illustrations in the colour section on pages v–xii will give you ideas on set and costume designers' use of colour.

Taurus mountains in Turkey
courtesy courteous behaviour

join in souls work together whole-heartedly
trim neat, fine

HELENA Nor none, in my mind, now you give her o'er.   135
LYSANDER Demetrius loves her, and he loves not you.
DEMETRIUS (*Waking.*)
        O Helen, goddess, nymph, perfect, divine!
        To what, my love, shall I compare thine eyne?
        Crystal is muddy! O, how ripe in show
        Thy lips, those kissing cherries, tempting grow!   140
        That pure congealèd white, high Taurus' snow,
        Fanned with the eastern wind, turns to a crow
        When thou hold'st up thy hand. O, let me kiss
        This princess of pure white, this seal of bliss!
HELENA O spite! O Hell! I see you all are bent   145
        To set against me for your merriment.
        If you were civil, and knew courtesy,
        You would not do me thus much injury.
        Can you not hate me, as I know you do,
        But you must join in souls to mock me too?   150
        If you were men, as men you are in show,
        You would not use a gentle lady so,
        To vow, and swear, and superpraise my parts,
        When I am sure you hate me with your hearts.
        You both are rivals, and love Hermia;   155
        And now both rivals to mock Helena.
        A trim exploit, a manly enterprise,
        To conjure tears up in a poor maid's eyes
        With your derision! None of noble sort
        Would so offend a virgin, and extort   160
        A poor soul's patience, all to make you sport.

Lysander and Demetrius argue over Helena. Hermia enters and asks Lysander why he left her. Lysander replies it is because he hates her.

1 The lovers at war (in groups of four)

Here 'reason and love' seem very far apart. 'Lovers' is hardly an apt description. There seem to be two arguments: one between Lysander and Demetrius, and the other between Hermia and Lysander.

Remember that the two men are under the influence of the flower juice's magic. But the two women do not suffer the same enchantment; they are bewildered by what's going on. Keep this notion of the difference between the state of the men and that of the women in mind as you work on the following activity.

Read through lines 162–91 for a first impression. Then repeat, emphasising the arguments as you see fit, and adding in the movements and gestures. Who, if anyone, has your sympathy, or whom do you laugh at? Why?

2 Onlookers – or voyeurs? (in small groups)

When you read the lovers' quarrels that now develop, it is easy to forget that Puck and Oberon are also on stage, watching. But when you see a performance their presence is always obvious (e.g. see photograph on p. 80).

This kind of voyeurism – watching the pain and confusion of others – does not reflect well on them. But are Puck and Oberon simply voyeurs? Explore the involvement and responses of Puck and Oberon. Do they move or stay still? Exchange glances with each other? With the audience? Try out ways of involving them in the action but not distracting from it.

bequeath give
guest-wise sojourned stayed for a while, like a visitor
Disparage speak badly of
Lest unless

aby pay for
apprehension understanding
engilds the night gives the night a golden sheen
oes bright dress ornaments (or stars)

LYSANDER You are unkind, Demetrius: be not so,
       For you love Hermia – this you know I know –
       And here with all good will, with all my heart,
       In Hermia's love I yield you up my part;   165
       And yours of Helena to me bequeath,
       Whom I do love, and will do till my death.
HELENA Never did mockers waste more idle breath.
DEMETRIUS Lysander, keep thy Hermia; I will none.
       If e'er I loved her, all that love is gone.   170
       My heart to her but as guest-wise sojourned,
       And now to Helen is it home returned,
       There to remain.
LYSANDER   Helen, it is not so.
DEMETRIUS Disparage not the faith thou dost not know,
       Lest to thy peril thou aby it dear.   175
       Look where thy love comes: yonder is thy dear.

Enter Hermia.

HERMIA Dark night, that from the eye his function takes,
       The ear more quick of apprehension makes;
       Wherein it doth impair the seeing sense
       It pays the hearing double recompense.   180
       Thou art not by mine eye, Lysander, found;
       Mine ear, I thank it, brought me to thy sound.
       But why unkindly didst thou leave me so?
LYSANDER Why should he stay whom love doth press to go?
HERMIA What love could press Lysander from my side?   185
LYSANDER Lysander's love, that would not let him bide,
       Fair Helena – who more engilds the night
       Than all yon fiery oes and eyes of light.
       [*To Hermia*] Why seek'st thou me? Could not this make
          thee know
       The hate I bare thee made me leave thee so?   190
HERMIA You speak not as you think; it cannot be.

Helena now thinks everyone is mocking her, and complains that Hermia should behave better as they have been such close friends for so long.

The lovers watched intently by Puck (sitting cross-legged in the background). Which line do you think is being spoken at this moment?

1 Sisterhood – under the pressure of love (in small groups)

Helena's speech raises the issue of loyalty between women. Speak it aloud, then discuss whether you think falling in love always puts a strain on female friendships. Pool your ideas on what emotions you think are at play in the female characters here. Then consider if those same feelings are present in female relationships today – and whether it is the same for men.

confederacy plot	**chid** scolded
Injurious wrongful, harmful	**sampler** piece of embroidery
bait torment	**incorporate** united in one body

HELENA Lo, she is one of this confederacy!
　　　　　Now I perceive they have conjoined all three
　　　　　To fashion this false sport in spite of me.
　　　　　Injurious Hermia, most ungrateful maid,　　　　　　195
　　　　　Have you conspired, have you with these contrived
　　　　　To bait me with this foul derision?
　　　　　Is all the counsel that we two have shared,
　　　　　The sisters' vows, the hours that we have spent
　　　　　When we have chid the hasty-footed time　　　　　200
　　　　　For parting us – O, is all forgot?
　　　　　All schooldays' friendship, childhood innocence?
　　　　　We, Hermia, like two artificial gods
　　　　　Have with our needles created both one flower,
　　　　　Both on one sampler, sitting on one cushion,　　　205
　　　　　Both warbling of one song, both in one key,
　　　　　As if our hands, our sides, voices, and minds
　　　　　Had been incorporate. So we grew together
　　　　　Like to a double cherry, seeming parted,
　　　　　But yet an union in partition,　　　　　　　　　210
　　　　　Two lovely berries moulded on one stem;
　　　　　So with two seeming bodies but one heart,
　　　　　Two of the first, like coats in heraldry,
　　　　　Due but to one, and crownèd with one crest.
　　　　　And will you rent our ancient love asunder,　　　215
　　　　　To join with men in scorning your poor friend?
　　　　　It is not friendly, 'tis not maidenly.
　　　　　Our sex, as well as I, may chide you for it,
　　　　　Though I alone do feel the injury.
HERMIA I am amazèd at your passionate words.　　　　　220
　　　　　I scorn you not; it seems that you scorn me.

Helena asks Hermia to have pity on her, and starts to leave because she's sure they are mocking her. Lysander offers to fight Demetrius for Helena.

1 Helena's bewilderment and distress (in pairs)

Helena, thoroughly confused by what's going on, makes three long speeches.

a Her first speech, lines 192–219, stresses what great friendship she and Hermia have always enjoyed. Work through it, identifying all the images of positive relationships and childhood. Which image strikes you as most powerfully conveying close friendship? Why?

b Helena's second speech, lines 222–35, accuses Hermia of setting on the two men to mock her, and appeals for pity. Take turns to speak the lines, bringing out Helena's accusatory tone as strongly as you can by stressing the words that most express her feelings.

c Her third speech, lines 237–44, is spoken to all three of the other characters. She accuses them all of laughing at her, condemns them for making her the subject of their 'sport', and prepares to leave, blaming herself. By this time Helena is probably very emotional, and may accompany all she says with gestures and facial expressions. Speak the lines using actions to illustrate their meaning.

2 Men fighting over women (in pairs)

In lines 248–56 the men begin to quarrel. The lines seem rather stereotyped and linked to the idea of male violence and male domination. They seem to indicate that things are getting out of control. Before you read on, briefly predict some of the ways in which this conflict could end.

forsooth   in truth
in grace   in favour
Persever   persevere, continue
counterfeit   pretend

Make mouths   pull faces
chronicled   told (as a funny story)
argument   subject (for making fun of)

HELENA Have you not set Lysander, as in scorn,
       To follow me, and praise my eyes and face?
       And made your other love, Demetrius,
       Who even but now did spurn me with his foot,   225
       To call me goddess, nymph, divine and rare,
       Precious, celestial? Wherefore speaks he this
       To her he hates? And wherefore doth Lysander
       Deny your love, so rich within his soul,
       And tender me, forsooth, affection,   230
       But by your setting on, by your consent?
       What though I be not so in grace as you,
       So hung upon with love, so fortunate,
       But miserable most, to love unloved:
       This you should pity rather than despise.   235
HERMIA I understand not what you mean by this.
HELENA Ay, do! Persever, counterfeit sad looks,
       Make mouths upon me when I turn my back,
       Wink each at other, hold the sweet jest up.
       This sport, well carried, shall be chronicled.   240
       If you have any pity, grace, or manners,
       You would not make me such an argument.
       But fare ye well. 'Tis partly my own fault,
       Which death or absence soon shall remedy.
LYSANDER Stay, gentle Helena: hear my excuse,   245
       My love, my life, my soul, fair Helena!
HELENA O, excellent!
HERMIA [To Lysander] Sweet, do not scorn her so.
DEMETRIUS If she cannot entreat, I can compel.
LYSANDER Thou canst compel no more than she entreat;
       Thy threats have no more strength than her weak prayers.   250
       Helen, I love thee, by my life, I do:
       I swear by that which I will lose for thee
       To prove him false that says I love thee not.
DEMETRIUS I say I love thee more than he can do.
LYSANDER If thou say so, withdraw, and prove it too.   255
DEMETRIUS Quick, come.

Hermia clings on to Lysander as he insults her and tells her that he hates her and loves Helena.

1 The quarrel – a read-through (in groups of four)

The quarrel between the lovers now really heats up. The episode provides wonderful entertainment in the theatre because, although it might seem very serious, it usually comes over as very funny. To gain a first impression of what happens, take parts and read lines 256–344. Don't pause over anything you can't understand – just enjoy the comedy. Afterwards, work on some of the activities.

2 Lysander's insults

Lysander's insults – 'Ethiop' and 'tawny Tartar' – sound extremely racist. The Elizabethans thought that a tan was unladylike and weather-beaten. Ladies didn't walk much in the open air – it was ordinary working people who had to be out in all weathers. If you were directing a production, would you omit these insults? Write a paragraph giving the reasons for your decision. On page 98 you will find an activity on the insults in the play.

3 Hermia's puzzlement – all questions (in pairs)

Now it is Hermia's turn to be bewildered by what's happening. She simply cannot understand why Lysander rejects and insults her. Most of what she says opposite is in the form of questions.

One person speaks all that Hermia says in the script opposite, pausing after each question. In the pause the other person repeats the question, exaggerating the questioning tone as forcefully as possible. Afterwards, count the number of questions and discuss why Shakespeare gives Hermia so many at this moment.

---

whereto tends all this? What do you mean?
tame lacking in spirit
burr prickly seed-case of a plant

bond oath, legal agreement
weak bond (Hermia's arms)
erewhile recently

HERMIA   Lysander, whereto tends all this?

LYSANDER Away, you Ethiop!

DEMETRIUS   No, no, sir,
  Seem to break loose, take on as you would follow,
  But yet come not. You are a tame man, go.

LYSANDER Hang off, thou cat, thou burr! Vile thing, let loose,   260
  Or I will shake thee from me like a serpent.

HERMIA Why are you grown so rude? What change is this,
  Sweet love?

LYSANDER   Thy love? – out, tawny Tartar, out;
  Out, loathed medicine! O hated potion, hence!

HERMIA Do you not jest?

HELENA   Yes, sooth, and so do you.   265

LYSANDER Demetrius, I will keep my word with thee.

DEMETRIUS I would I had your bond, for I perceive
  A weak bond holds you. I'll not trust your word.

LYSANDER What? Should I hurt her, strike her, kill her dead?
  Although I hate her, I'll not harm her so.   270

HERMIA What? Can you do me greater harm than hate?
  Hate me? Wherefore? O me, what news, my love?
  Am not I Hermia? Are not you Lysander?
  I am as fair now as I was erewhile.
  Since night you loved me; yet since night you left me.   275
  Why then, you left me – O, the gods forbid! –
  In earnest, shall I say?

LYSANDER   Ay, by my life;
  And never did desire to see thee more.
  Therefore be out of hope, of question, of doubt;
  Be certain, nothing truer – 'tis no jest   280
  That I do hate thee and love Helena.

Hermia turns on Helena and threatens to fight her, thinking Helena has stolen Lysander's love. Helena says she will return to Athens.

1 The women quarrel (in pairs)

Hermia's puzzlement now turns to anger, and she directs her rage at Helena, accusing her of having stolen Lysander's love. Hermia's accusation arouses Helena's indignation, and she responds with similar passion (notice again how Shakespeare is showing how 'reason and love keep little company').

First, take parts and speak all the two women say between lines 282 and 344 (leave out the men's speeches in this activity). Then talk together about the following.

a **Insults**   It seems as if Hermia is angered by Helena insulting her ('Puppet') because she is short. She returns the insult, calling Helena 'thou painted maypole'. Identify all the other 'height' words or phrases that are used, then discuss the attitudes current today about being short and being tall. Decide whether those attitudes are similar to the attitudes expressed by Helena and Hermia. Could an equivalent argument happen today?

b **Fighting**   'Let her not strike me.' The two women seem very close to fighting physically. Do your reactions to this differ from your reactions to the probability of the men fighting – and if so, why? In the play, is it purely for humour, or are there sinister undertones as well?

c **Love conceals, anger reveals**   Consider whether or not the characters of Hermia and Helena are revealed more clearly here than in all their previous scenes (where only their love seemed to be apparent). Their relationship now appears more complicated – how would you describe it?

---

canker-blossom   diseased flower
counterfeit   cheat
prevailed with him   won Lysander's
  love

curst   fierce
shrewishness   anger, scolding
chid   scolded, rebuked

HERMIA [*To Helena*]
    O me, you juggler, you canker-blossom,
    You thief of love! What, have you come by night
    And stol'n my love's heart from him?
HELENA   Fine, i'faith!
    Have you no modesty, no maiden shame,   285
    No touch of bashfulness? What, will you tear
    Impatient answers from my gentle tongue?
    Fie, fie, you counterfeit, you puppet, you!
HERMIA 'Puppet'? Why so? – Ay, that way goes the game.
    Now I perceive that she hath made compare   290
    Between our statures; she hath urged her height,
    And with her personage, her tall personage,
    Her height, forsooth, she hath prevailed with him.
    And are you grown so high in his esteem
    Because I am so dwarfish and so low?   295
    How low am I, thou painted maypole? Speak!
    How low am I? I am not yet so low
    But that my nails can reach unto thine eyes.
HELENA I pray you, though you mock me, gentlemen,
    Let her not hurt me. I was never curst;   300
    I have no gift at all in shrewishness.
    I am a right maid for my cowardice;
    Let her not strike me. You perhaps may think
    Because she is something lower than myself
    That I can match her.
HERMIA   Lower? Hark, again!   305
HELENA Good Hermia, do not be so bitter with me.
    I evermore did love you, Hermia,
    Did ever keep your counsels, never wronged you,
    Save that in love unto Demetrius
    I told him of your stealth unto this wood.   310
    He followed you; for love I followed him,
    But he hath chid me hence, and threatened me
    To strike me, spurn me, nay, to kill me too.
    And now, so you will let me quiet go,
    To Athens will I bear my folly back,   315
    And follow you no further. Let me go;
    You see how simple and how fond I am.

Helena explains her fear of 'little' Hermia. Lysander and Demetrius leave to fight. Helena runs away, and Hermia follows.

---

1 How much of a scuffle? (in groups of four)

The lovers' quarrels end very dramatically. Love, hate, hurt, jealousy and aggression all mingle in lines 318–44. It's all very physical, with plenty of insults. The lines contain many implied stage directions, so use the clues in the language to work out what each character does: who stands where, movements, who speaks to whom, how characters go off stage and so on. Act out the lines using the picture below, the picture on page ix (top) in the colour section and the picture on page 80 for inspiration.

minimus insignificant creature	**cheek by jowl** face to face
knot-grass a weed which was thought	**coil** turmoil
to stunt growth	**'long** because of
aby pay for	**fray** fight

HERMIA Why, get you gone! Who is't that hinders you?
HELENA A foolish heart that I leave here behind.
HERMIA What, with Lysander?
HELENA   With Demetrius.   320
LYSANDER Be not afraid; she shall not harm thee, Helena.
DEMETRIUS No, sir. She shall not, though you take her part.
HELENA O, when she is angry she is keen and shrewd;
              She was a vixen when she went to school,
              And though she be but little, she is fierce.   325
HERMIA Little again? Nothing but low and little?
              Why will you suffer her to flout me thus?
              Let me come to her.
LYSANDER   Get you gone, you dwarf,
              You minimus of hindering knot-grass made,
              You bead, you acorn.
DEMETRIUS   You are too officious   330
              In her behalf that scorns your services.
              Let her alone: speak not of Helena,
              Take not her part; for if thou dost intend
              Never so little show of love to her,
              Thou shalt aby it.
LYSANDER   Now she holds me not –   335
              Now follow, if thou dur'st, to try whose right,
              Of thine or mine, is most in Helena.
DEMETRIUS Follow? Nay, I'll go with thee, cheek by jowl.
                              Exeunt Lysander and Demetrius
HERMIA You, mistress, all this coil is 'long of you.
              Nay, go not back.
HELENA   I will not trust you, I,   340
              Nor longer stay in your curst company.
              Your hands than mine are quicker for a fray;
              My legs are longer, though, to run away!   [*Exit*]
HERMIA I am amazed, and know not what to say.   *Exit*

Puck explains his mistake. Oberon orders him to lead Lysander and Demetrius astray by imitating their voices. He will 'beg' the Indian boy from Titania, then release her from the charm and put all things right.

---

1 Focus on Oberon and Puck (in pairs)

Puck and Oberon now share the scene's next episode, in lines 345–95. To gain a first impression, take parts and speak the lines. Afterwards, work on the following.

a **Master and servant**   Talk together about how, in performance, you would show the relationship between the two fairy characters.

b **Oberon the peacemaker**   Consider the photograph on page 92. Talk about whether it suggests that Oberon has Christ-like qualities and wishes to bring about love and harmony. Use evidence from the script to support your views.

c **Reactions**   During a long speech the other actor on stage has the problem of reacting but saying nothing. Take turns to speak Oberon's lines opposite while the other responds. Puck's responses can be as subtle or as physical as you wish. Choose your favourite reaction and share it with the class.

d **A promised restoration of order?**   Compare the language and imagery of lines 354–95 with the writing earlier in the scene, such as lines 257–305. The power of some of the images here seems to change how you are invited to look at events (e.g. line 371 'seem a dream and fruitless vision'). Think about the audience and discuss how they might react to the suggestion that everything that has happened might seem like just a dream, a kind of surreal parallel universe that Shakespeare is conjuring up.

---

sort   turn out
welkin   sky
Acheron   one of the rivers in Hades, the underworld for the dead
testy   bad-tempered
bitter wrong   sharp accusations

rail   use abusive language
wonted   usual
derision   stupidity
league   contract, agreement
date   duration

Oberon and Puck come forward.

OBERON This is thy negligence. Still thou mistak'st,   345
        Or else committ'st thy knaveries wilfully.

PUCK Believe me, King of Shadows, I mistook.
        Did not you tell me I should know the man
        By the Athenian garments he had on?
        And so far blameless proves my enterprise   350
        That I have 'nointed an Athenian's eyes;
        And so far am I glad it so did sort,
        As this their jangling I esteem a sport.

OBERON Thou seest these lovers seek a place to fight:
        Hie therefore, Robin, overcast the night;   355
        The starry welkin cover thou anon
        With drooping fog as black as Acheron,
        And lead these testy rivals so astray
        As one come not within another's way.
        Like to Lysander sometime frame thy tongue,   360
        Then stir Demetrius up with bitter wrong,
        And sometime rail thou like Demetrius;
        And from each other look thou lead them thus,
        Till o'er their brows death-counterfeiting sleep
        With leaden legs and batty wings doth creep.   365
        Then crush this herb into Lysander's eye,
        Whose liquor hath this virtuous property,
        To take from thence all error with his might,
        And make his eyeballs roll with wonted sight.
        When they next wake, all this derision   370
        Shall seem a dream and fruitless vision,
        And back to Athens shall the lovers wend
        With league whose date till death shall never end.
        Whiles I in this affair do thee employ
        I'll to my Queen and beg her Indian boy;   375
        And then I will her charmèd eye release
        From monster's view, and all things shall be peace.

Day approaches, and though the fairies (unlike other spirits) can exist in the day, Oberon urges haste. Puck looks forward to misleading the lovers. Lysander returns and Puck deceives him.

Puck and Oberon. What line might be spoken here?

Aurora's harbinger   signal of the dawn – the morning star
aye   ever
consort   keep company

Neptune   god of the sea. The morning sun's beams turn the sea from green to 'yellow gold', transforming it
drawn   with drawn sword
plainer   more open

PUCK   My fairy lord, this must be done with haste,
        For night's swift dragons cut the clouds full fast,
        And yonder shines Aurora's harbinger,   380
        At whose approach ghosts wandering here and there
        Troop home to churchyards. Damnèd spirits all,
        That in crossways and floods have burial,
        Already to their wormy beds are gone.
        For fear lest day should look their shames upon,   385
        They wilfully themselves exile from light,
        And must for aye consort with black-browed night.
OBERON   But we are spirits of another sort.
        I with the morning's love have oft made sport,
        And like a forester the groves may tread   390
        Even till the eastern gate, all fiery-red,
        Opening on Neptune with fair blessèd beams,
        Turns into yellow gold his salt green streams.
        But notwithstanding, haste, make no delay;
        We may effect this business yet ere day.   *[Exit]* 395
PUCK   Up and down, up and down,
            I will lead them up and down;
            I am feared in field and town.
            Goblin, lead them up and down.
        Here comes one.   400

Enter Lysander.

LYSANDER   Where art thou, proud Demetrius? Speak thou now.
PUCK   Here, villain, drawn and ready! Where art thou?
LYSANDER   I will be with thee straight.
PUCK   Follow me then
        To plainer ground.

                       [Exit Lysander]

Puck misleads both Demetrius and Lysander by imitating their voices. Both men finally have had enough and fall asleep.

---

1 Sleep sound (in groups of five)

The final episode of Scene 2 shows Puck misleading the two men until they sleep, then watching the two women enter and sleep, and finally squeezing the love juice into Lysander's eyes. Once again, it is best to gain a first impression by taking parts, reading from line 401 to the end of the scene. Then work on the activities provided.

a **Imitation**   Consider how Puck should imitate Lysander's voice well enough to fool Demetrius (and, a little later, imitate Demetrius's own voice). Discuss the different dramatic effects of using good imitation and obviously inaccurate imitation.

b **Direct the lovers**   Work out how to get all the lovers asleep near one another. Remember that Lysander must sleep near Hermia, so that he loves her when he wakes. The stage direction simply reads *Sleeps*, but in many productions Puck takes a very direct (and often very funny) part in getting the lovers to sleep near their partners.

c **Men versus women**   Compare the speeches of the male lovers with those of the female lovers. Talk together about how they differ from or resemble each other. Activity 2 on page 96 (on what Puck says) may help you.

d **What set for sleepers?**   There's a lot of sleeping in the play and this could cause practical problems on stage. If you were directing, would you want actors to sleep on the bare stage floor, or would you want a set that offered more comfortable options such as mossy banks or fairy glades? Talk together about the problems and the solutions, and then sketch or write your ideas for a set that accommodates the sleeping lovers.

---

recreant   coward, villain
defiled   made dirty
lighter-heeled   faster
Abide   face

wot   know
buy this dear   suffer, pay dearly
To measure out my length   to lie down

94

Enter Demetrius.

DEMETRIUS   Lysander, speak again.
        Thou runaway, thou coward, art thou fled?   405
        Speak! In some bush? Where dost thou hide thy head?
PUCK Thou coward, art thou bragging to the stars,
        Telling the bushes that thou look'st for wars,
        And wilt not come? Come, recreant, come, thou child,
        I'll whip thee with a rod. He is defiled   410
        That draws a sword on thee.
DEMETRIUS   Yea, art thou there?
PUCK Follow my voice. We'll try no manhood here.

                                                    Exeunt

            [*Enter Lysander.*]

LYSANDER He goes before me, and still dares me on;
        When I come where he calls, then he is gone.
        The villain is much lighter-heeled than I;   415
        I followed fast, but faster he did fly,
        That fallen am I in dark uneven way,
        And here will rest me. (*Lies down.*) Come, thou gentle day,
        For if but once thou show me thy grey light
        I'll find Demetrius and revenge this spite. [*Sleeps.*]   420

            Enter Puck and Demetrius.

PUCK Ho, ho, ho! Coward, why com'st thou not?
DEMETRIUS Abide me if thou dar'st, for well I wot
        Thou runn'st before me, shifting every place,
        And dar'st not stand nor look me in the face.
        Where art thou now?
PUCK   Come hither; I am here.   425
DEMETRIUS Nay then, thou mock'st me. Thou shalt buy this dear
        If ever I thy face by daylight see.
        Now, go thy way; faintness constraineth me
        To measure out my length on this cold bed.
        By day's approach look to be visited. [*Sleeps.*]   430

Helena and Hermia enter separately, exhausted, and fall asleep. Puck puts the magic juice on Lysander's eyes to make him love Hermia again.

1 Rhymes – mortals and fairies (in groups of three)

The final two episodes of this scene (from line 350) have been in rhyming verse. The rhymes are particularly obvious in the script opposite. In Shakespeare's day 'east' could rhyme with 'detest'. You may have done an earlier activity on rhyme (p. 48), and here is an opportunity to go further.

Take parts and speak the script opposite, emphasising the rhymes. Then talk together about whether Puck (a fairy) can more convincingly stress the rhymes than Hermia and Helena (mortals). What would be your advice to the actors here?

2 Puck – on women and love

Read what Puck says about women in lines 439–41 and 453–63. Write a paragraph on the attitude he seems to have towards them.

3 To sleep, perchance to dream

Although there has been a night and dreams, at the end of the scene the lovers are asleep. Write down the thoughts and feelings of each as they drift into sleep. Alternatively, write about their dreams.

4 Improvise an awakening (in groups of four)

Improvise a scene immediately following this, in which the lovers wake up and discover that they are now neatly sorted out into couples. How confused or amazed are they? What do they remember? How do they decipher the 'dream' from reality? You will find out how Shakespeare dramatises the wakening in the next act.

Abate diminish, cut short
curst bad-tempered
Bedabbled stained

Jack shall have Jill . . . The man shall have his mare again proverbs of Shakespeare's time for 'boy gets girl'

Enter Helena.

HELENA O weary night, O long and tedious night,
     Abate thy hours, shine comforts from the east,
  That I may back to Athens by daylight
     From these that my poor company detest;
  And sleep, that sometimes shuts up sorrow's eye,   435
  Steal me awhile from mine own company. (*Sleeps.*)

PUCK   Yet but three? Come one more,
     Two of both kinds makes up four.
     Here she comes, curst and sad.
     Cupid is a knavish lad   440
     Thus to make poor females mad.

Enter Hermia.

HERMIA Never so weary, never so in woe,
     Bedabbled with the dew, and torn with briars –
  I can no further crawl, no further go;
     My legs can keep no pace with my desires.   445
  Here will I rest me till the break of day.
  Heavens shield Lysander, if they mean a fray. [*Sleeps.*]

PUCK   On the ground
     Sleep sound.
     I'll apply   450
     To your eye,
    Gentle lover, remedy.
    [*Squeezes the juice on Lysander's eyes.*]
     When thou wak'st,
     Thou tak'st
     True delight   455
     In the sight
     Of thy former lady's eye;
    And the country proverb known,
    That every man should take his own,
  In your waking shall be shown.   460
     Jack shall have Jill,
     Naught shall go ill:
  The man shall have his mare again, and all shall be well.
     [*Exit Puck;*] *the lovers remain on stage, asleep*

Looking back at Act 3
Activities for groups or individuals

1 Midsummer dream – or nightmare?

Below is a version of a famous 'nightmare' picture. There are many nightmarish things about this play – being turned into an ass, and Hermia's nightmare of the snake, are two. Describe, paint or draw a memorable dream you have had. Then, in groups, relate your dreams and nightmares, and see if you can find meaning in them. Discuss whether you believe dreams have any significance.

The Scream by Edvard Munch.

2 What an insult!

Scene 2 contains plenty of insults, and there are quite a few others in the play. Make a list of all the insults you can find in Act 3, number them and share them out amongst a group, one each. Learn your insult by heart and practise speaking it in a variety of ways. Then walk around, with each group member insulting the others. Afterwards, the group chooses four or five of their favourite insults and uses them as a basis for an improvisation.

3 Transformation

There are many myths about people being transformed into animals, including asses. Bottom is something of an ass (fool) already. Some people have seen a darker side to his transformation to a real ass, associating the ass with sexual prowess. Others see it as a mockery of romance. Thinking about this, look at the pictures on page viii of the colour section and pages 62, 64, 66 and 156. Which do you prefer? Why?

4 The world of the wood

Use some of the following to help you visualise the play.

a **A map**   Devise a map of Athens and the wood. The play hints at locations, but think about Titania's bower in relation to the Mechanicals' rehearsal space. Also insert where the various lovers' scenes might take place. Remember that the Mechanicals don't meet the lovers in the wood.

b **A website**   Design a website for 'a wood near Athens'. Your aim is to attract tourists.

c **A display**   Create a display that shows how you think the world of the woods should look on stage or film. You could use drawings, photographs and other images.

d **A board game**   Develop a board game based on *A Midsummer Night's Dream*.

e **A stage set**   For professional stage productions, designers always make a detailed model set before proceeding to the full-sized version. Design (or write about) your own stage set for the wood scenes.

f **A costume design**   Design costumes for the fairy world. There is much imagery that connects the natural world and the woodland, in particular with the fairies. Use this connection to help your thinking about costume and colour. As you design costumes for the fairy world, think of contrasting dress for the Mechanicals, the lovers and the court.

Titania speaks lovingly to Bottom. He gives instructions to her fairies to scratch him and find him food.

Bottom, Titania and the fairies. Identify the differences between the picture above and the ones in the colour section and on pages 102 and 170. Begin with costume and expression. Talk together about the mood or feeling that you think each production created for the fairy world.

1 How has Bottom changed? (in pairs)

Bottom gives all kinds of detailed orders to the fairies. On stage his style of speaking is often very different from that in his earlier appearances, although there are some similarities. Take turns to speak his lines, then compile a list of ways in which you think he has changed. Suggest how these changes might be clearly presented in performance.

coy caress
neaf hand
Cavalery a gentleman (Bottom's mistake for 'cavalier')

tongs and the bones simple musical instruments
a peck of provender a little food
bottle bundle

Act 4 Scene 1
The wood

Enter TITANIA, Queen of Fairies, and BOTTOM, and fairies
[including PEASEBLOSSOM, COBWEB and MUSTARDSEED;] and
the King OBERON behind them.

TITANIA Come, sit thee down upon this flowery bed
    While I thy amiable cheeks do coy,
    And stick musk-roses in thy sleek smooth head,
    And kiss thy fair large ears, my gentle joy.

BOTTOM Where's Peaseblossom? 5

PEASEBLOSSOM Ready.

BOTTOM Scratch my head, Peaseblossom. Where's Mounsieur
Cobweb?

COBWEB Ready.

BOTTOM Mounsieur Cobweb, good Mounsieur, get you your weapons 10
in your hand, and kill me a red-hipped humble-bee on the top of
a thistle; and, good Mounsieur, bring me the honey-bag. Do not
fret yourself too much in the action, Mounsieur; and, good
Mounsieur, have a care the honey-bag break not; I would be loath
to have you overflown with a honey-bag, signior. Where's Moun- 15
sieur Mustardseed?

MUSTARDSEED Ready.

BOTTOM Give me your neaf, Mounsieur Mustardseed. Pray you, leave
your courtesy, good Mounsieur.

MUSTARDSEED What's your will? 20

BOTTOM Nothing, good Mounsieur, but to help Cavalery Peaseblossom
to scratch. I must to the barber's, Mounsieur, for methinks I am
marvellous hairy about the face. And I am such a tender ass, if my
hair do but tickle me, I must scratch.

TITANIA What, wilt thou hear some music, my sweet love? 25

BOTTOM I have a reasonable good ear in music. Let's have the tongs
and the bones.

TITANIA Or say, sweet love, what thou desir'st to eat.

BOTTOM Truly, a peck of provender, I could munch your good dry oats.
Methinks I have a great desire to a bottle of hay. Good hay, sweet 30
hay hath no fellow.

Bottom and Titania sleep. Oberon talks to Puck about his pity for Titania, and how she has returned the changeling boy. He removes the spell from her.

Bottom says that he is sleepy. How does he react to Titania's lines 37–42? For example, he might look at her lovingly. Or he might appear complacent and self-satisfied. In some productions he ogles her suggestively. In one he was already asleep! Make your suggestions about how you think he responds to her loving words.

1 Seeing versus hearing – and 'sweet sight' (in small groups)

Oberon's speech is full of vivid descriptions and actions.

a One person reads lines 43–67 while the others mime the actions described. Which do you feel is more effective: hearing and seeing, or just hearing and imagining?

b Oberon calls what he sees a 'sweet sight' (line 43). Talk together about whether he really means what he says, and the tone in which he speaks 'sweet sight'.

exposition of another of Bottom's mistakes. Surely he means disposition to?
woodbine bindweed

dotage foolishness
orient lustrous, eastern
swain lover

TITANIA I have a venturous fairy that shall seek
        The squirrel's hoard, and fetch thee new nuts.

BOTTOM I had rather have a handful or two of dried peas. But, I pray
        you, let none of your people stir me; I have an exposition of sleep   35
        come upon me.

TITANIA Sleep thou, and I will wind thee in my arms.
        Fairies be gone, and be all ways away.

                                [*Exeunt Fairies*]

        So doth the woodbine the sweet honeysuckle
        Gently entwist; the female ivy so   40
        Enrings the barky fingers of the elm.
        O, how I love thee! How I dote on thee!

        [*They sleep.*]

        Enter PUCK.

OBERON [*Coming forward.*]
        Welcome, good Robin. Seest thou this sweet sight?
        Her dotage now I do begin to pity;
        For, meeting her of late behind the wood   45
        Seeking sweet favours for this hateful fool,
        I did upbraid her and fall out with her,
        For she his hairy temples then had rounded
        With coronet of fresh and fragrant flowers;
        And that same dew, which sometime on the buds   50
        Was wont to swell like round and orient pearls,
        Stood now within the pretty flowerets' eyes
        Like tears that did their own disgrace bewail.
        When I had at my pleasure taunted her,
        And she in mild terms begged my patience,   55
        I then did ask of her her changeling child,
        Which straight she gave me, and her fairy sent
        To bear him to my bower in Fairyland.
        And now I have the boy, I will undo
        This hateful imperfection of her eyes.   60
        And, gentle Puck, take this transformèd scalp
        From off the head of this Athenian swain,
        That, he awaking when the other do,
        May all to Athens back again repair,
        And think no more of this night's accidents   65
        But as the fierce vexation of a dream.
        But first I will release the Fairy Queen.

        [*Squeezing a herb on Titania's eyes.*]

Titania wakes, and she and Oberon are reconciled. Puck removes the ass's head from Bottom. All leave except the 'mortals' (the lovers and Bottom).

1 Music and dance = harmony (in pairs)

The resolution of the conflict between Titania and Oberon is marked by both dance and music. In Elizabethan times, the harmony of music was often taken as a symbol of human harmony. The music and dance in modern productions vary widely. Sometimes they are formal and dignified, sometimes wildly extravagant.

What kind of music and dance do you think is suitable for this moment in the play? Try to find time to develop a short dance for Titania and Oberon, perhaps to some appropriate music you have found, or have created yourselves.

2 Many sleepers on stage

The four lovers have been asleep on stage all this time, and Bottom also has been asleep since line 42. Oberon refers to them as 'all these five' (line 79). If the stage is small, it can create problems for the actors: the dance (which sometimes involves all the fairies) must take place without falling over the sleepers. Look back at Activities 4b and d on page 94 and think again about how you would position the sleepers on stage. Sketch your solution.

3 A change in Oberon's language (in pairs)

Oberon's language between lines 82 and 95 is markedly different in style, tone and meaning from his first speeches in Act 2 Scene 1, lines 60–80. Suggest possible reasons for this change. Also discuss whether you think that Shakespeare is using his fairy characters here as a guide to how human beings should behave towards each other.

---

wast wont used, was accustomed
Dian's bud (possibly the antidote to Cupid's flower)
amity friendly relations
compass go round

Be as thou wast wont to be;
See as thou wast wont to see.
Dian's bud o'er Cupid's flower   70
Hath such force and blessèd power.
Now, my Titania, wake you, my sweet Queen!

TITANIA [*Starting up.*]
My Oberon, what visions have I seen!
Methought I was enamoured of an ass.

OBERON There lies your love.

TITANIA   How came these things to pass?   75
O, how mine eyes do loathe his visage now!

OBERON Silence awhile: Robin, take off this head.
Titania, music call, and strike more dead
Than common sleep of all these five the sense.

TITANIA Music, ho, music such as charmeth sleep!   80
                    [*Soft music plays.*]

PUCK [*To Bottom, removing the ass's head*]
Now when thou wak'st, with thine own fool's eyes peep.

OBERON Sound, music! Come, my Queen, take hands with me,
And rock the ground whereon these sleepers be.
                    [*They dance.*]
Now thou and I are new in amity,
And will tomorrow midnight solemnly   85
Dance in Duke Theseus' house triumphantly,
And bless it to all fair prosperity.
There shall the pairs of faithful lovers be
Wedded, with Theseus, all in jollity.

PUCK   Fairy King, attend, and mark: 90
I do hear the morning lark.

OBERON   Then, my Queen, in silence sad,
Trip we after night's shade;
We the globe can compass soon,
Swifter than the wandering moon.   95

TITANIA   Come, my lord, and in our flight
Tell me how it came this night
That I sleeping here was found
With these mortals on the ground.
                    Exeunt Oberon, Titania and Puck

Theseus, Hippolyta and the others enter, on an early morning hunting expedition. After praising the baying of the hounds, they find the sleeping lovers.

---

1 From night to day

The transition between the exit of the fairies at line 99 and the entrance of the court moves the action from the fairy world of moonlight to the daylight world of Theseus. Write a paragraph saying how you would signal this change on stage in a dramatically effective way.

2 In praise of hunting dogs (in pairs)

Theseus's and Hippolyta's speeches about the hounds may sound unfamiliar to a modern audience. Take parts and speak lines 100–23, then discuss how you think the lines could be delivered on stage to engage the imagination and interest of the audience.

3 Theseus – a joke? And a warning? (in pairs)

a 'The rite of May' line 130) connects with the festivals of Tudor England (as does the title of the play itself). In some of these festivals, ordinary behaviour and laws were dispensed with. Such festivals celebrated disorder and allowed people to behave in a way that was free of ordinary constraints. In performance, Theseus's lines 129–30 often evoke audience laughter. Talk together about whether you think that is an appropriate response – and why.

b A word of warning? Are lines 132–4 a menacing moment because of the sudden remembrance of the threat to put Hermia in a convent or execute her? Suggest how Theseus might speak these lines. Also discuss whether it makes you doubt a happy ending. If not, why not?

---

vaward early part
Uncouple unleash them
Cadmus mythical founder of Thebes
So flewed, so sanded with similar jowls and similar sandy colouring

dewlapped with loose neck skin
matched in mouth like bells loud like bells

Wind horns. Enter THESEUS *with* HIPPOLYTA, EGEUS, *and all his train.*

THESEUS Go, one of you, find out the forester;   100
      For now our observation is performed,
      And since we have the vaward of the day,
      My love shall hear the music of my hounds.
      Uncouple in the western valley; let them go:
      Dispatch, I say, and find the forester.   105
                              [Exit an Attendant]
      We will, fair Queen, up to the mountain's top,
      And mark the musical confusion
      Of hounds and echo in conjunction.
HIPPOLYTA I was with Hercules and Cadmus once,
      When in a wood of Crete they bayed the bear   110
      With hounds of Sparta: never did I hear
      Such gallant chiding; for besides the groves,
      The skies, the fountains, every region near
      Seemed all one mutual cry. I never heard
      So musical a discord, such sweet thunder.   115
THESEUS My hounds are bred out of the Spartan kind,
      So flewed, so sanded; and their heads are hung
      With ears that sweep away the morning dew;
      Crook-kneed, and dewlapped like Thessalian bulls;
      Slow in pursuit, but matched in mouth like bells,   120
      Each under each. A cry more tuneable
      Was never hallooed to nor cheered with horn
      In Crete, in Sparta, nor in Thessaly.
      Judge when you hear. But soft, what nymphs are these?
EGEUS My lord, this is my daughter here asleep,   125
      And this Lysander; this Demetrius is,
      This Helena, old Nedar's Helena.
      I wonder of their being here together.
THESEUS No doubt they rose up early to observe
      The rite of May, and hearing our intent   130
      Came here in grace of our solemnity.
      But speak, Egeus; is not this the day
      That Hermia should give answer of her choice?
EGEUS It is, my lord.

The lovers are woken by shouts and blasts on horns. Lysander tries to explain what has happened. Egeus urges the duke to punish Lysander for attempting to elope with Hermia.

1 The dance of lovers – who loves whom? (IV)

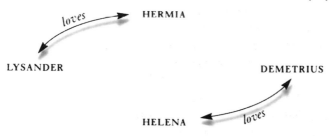

This is the final arrangement of the lovers. Look back at the 'dance' of the lovers on pages 10, 50 and 76. Putting all the dances together, identify what pattern emerges. When you have read to the end of the play, you could apply this method to look for patterns of day/night, Athens/wood, and others. Make charts, graphs or displays of your findings.

2 Just how do they awake?

The lovers '*all start up*'. But how? Puck has ensured that when each awakes they will first see the person they love. Put the stage direction into action by acting out their wakening. They see first their lover, then Theseus and his court – with Egeus.

3 Egeus – still an angry father

Egeus, having not experienced the night's 'dreams', continues to view the world as one in conflict (see activity on p. 116). He continues to demand his legal rights as an Athenian father. For him the 'dream' has had no effect on the real world.

This is the last time Egeus speaks in the play. What are your final thoughts on him? Write a brief character sketch as a guide for an actor preparing to play this part.

Saint Valentine (a popular belief was   **couple** pair up
that birds chose their mates on   **Without** beyond
St Valentine's Day)   **defeated** cheated

THESEUS Go, bid the huntsmen wake them with their horns.   135
        Shout within; wind horns; [the lovers] all start up.
    Good morrow, friends. Saint Valentine is past;
    Begin these woodbirds but to couple now?
             [The lovers kneel.]
LYSANDER Pardon, my lord.
THESEUS   I pray you all, stand up.
    I know you two are rival enemies:
    How comes this gentle concord in the world,   140
    That hatred is so far from jealousy
    To sleep by hate, and fear no enmity?
LYSANDER My lord, I shall reply amazedly,
    Half sleep, half waking; but as yet, I swear,
    I cannot truly say how I came here.   145
    But as I think (for truly would I speak)
    And now I do bethink me, so it is –
    I came with Hermia hither. Our intent
    Was to be gone from Athens, where we might
    Without the peril of the Athenian law –   150
EGEUS Enough, enough, my lord; you have enough –
    I beg the law, the law upon his head!
    They would have stol'n away, they would, Demetrius,
    Thereby to have defeated you and me,
    You of your wife, and me of my consent,   155
    Of my consent that she should be your wife.

Demetrius explains his love for Hermia has melted and he loves Helena, now and evermore. Theseus instructs the lovers to come with him to be married. All leave except the lovers.

1 Demetrius – has he changed? (in pairs)

Compare Demetrius's speech opposite with one of his earlier speeches. Pick one speech each, and read one, then the other, trying to bring out Demetrius's mood and character. How has he changed – and why?

2 Romantic and heartfelt

a Demetrius's lines 172–3 are very emotional:

> Now I do wish it, love it, long for it,
> And will for evermore be true to it.

Will speeches such as this make all Helena's suffering and humiliation worthwhile for her? Write a paragraph saying how she feels at this point.

b Theseus made a joke about St Valentine's Day at line 136. *A Midsummer Night's Dream* is a romantic comedy full of beautiful verse. Which lines in the play would make appropriate verses for a Valentine Day's card? Design your card with a dream theme, using a quotation from the play.

3 Dominant men? (in small groups)

At this moment Theseus is the dominant character. Read his speeches in this scene aloud, then speak Oberon's earlier in the scene. Afterwards, talk together about and list the similarities and differences between the two characters. Also discuss whether you think the fairy and mortal worlds are totally dominated by men, or whether the men's power is limited in certain ways. You will find an activity on Titania and Hippolyta on page 116.

---

in fancy doting, in love
wot know
idle gaud worthless toy
overbear your will overrule your wishes

something worn somewhat spent, nearly over

DEMETRIUS My lord, fair Helen told me of their stealth,
　　　　　Of this their purpose hither to this wood;
　　　　　And I in fury hither followed them,
　　　　　Fair Helena in fancy following me.　　　　　　　　　160
　　　　　But, my good lord, I wot not by what power
　　　　　(But by some power it is), my love to Hermia,
　　　　　Melted as the snow, seems to me now
　　　　　As the remembrance of an idle gaud
　　　　　Which in my childhood I did dote upon;　　　　　　165
　　　　　And all the faith, the virtue of my heart,
　　　　　The object and the pleasure of mine eye,
　　　　　Is only Helena. To her, my lord,
　　　　　Was I betrothed ere I saw Hermia;
　　　　　But like a sickness did I loathe this food.　　　　　170
　　　　　But, as in health come to my natural taste,
　　　　　Now I do wish it, love it, long for it,
　　　　　And will for evermore be true to it.
THESEUS Fair lovers, you are fortunately met.
　　　　　Of this discourse we more will hear anon.　　　　　175
　　　　　Egeus, I will overbear your will;
　　　　　For in the temple, by and by, with us
　　　　　These couples shall eternally be knit.
　　　　　And, for the morning now is something worn,
　　　　　Our purposed hunting shall be set aside.　　　　　180
　　　　　Away with us to Athens. Three and three,
　　　　　We'll hold a feast in great solemnity.
　　　　　Come, Hippolyta.
　　　　　　　　　Exit Theseus with Hippolyta, Egeus, and his train

The lovers wonder if they are dreaming, agree they are awake, and follow the duke. Bottom wakes, and wonders at his 'dream'.

1 Reflections on dreaming (in groups of five)

In the script opposite, first the lovers, then Bottom, reflect on the 'dream' they have experienced. Take parts and speak the lines, then work on some of the following activities.

a Talk together about the different ways in which the lovers and Bottom describe their experiences. Consider each speech in turn and suggest how it could be delivered on stage.

b Demetrius says 'let us recount our dreams' as they walk back to Athens. In role, do just that. Each character tells not only what they think happened, but also what they have learned.

c Identify the lines in Bottom's speech which have similarities with this passage in the Bible: I Corinthians 2.9:

> But as it is written, Eye hath not seen, nor ear heard, neither have entered into the heart of man, the things which God hath prepared for them that love him.

d Bottom says he will get Peter Quince to write a ballad called 'Bottom's Dream'. Write and perform your own version of the ballad.

e Bottom appears to be at his most philosophical here. What might he have learned about love, life and himself? Question the person who has been reading the part of Bottom about what his dream has taught him.

f Act out a television news report with interviews of the lovers and Bottom.

g Become newspaper reporters. Interview the five characters. Write two reports: one in the style of a popular newspaper that prints scandal, the other in the style of a serious newspaper.

---

patched fool   a Fool (who wore a traditional patchwork costume)
ballad   a simple song

Peradventure   perhaps
her death   (referring to Thisbe in the Mechanicals' play)

DEMETRIUS These things seem small and undistinguishable,
    Like far-off mountains turnèd into clouds.   185
HERMIA Methinks I see these things with parted eye,
    When everything seems double.
HELENA   So methinks;
    And I have found Demetrius, like a jewel,
    Mine own, and not mine own.
DEMETRIUS   Are you sure
    That we are awake? It seems to me   190
    That yet we sleep, we dream. Do not you think
    The Duke was here, and bid us follow him?
HERMIA Yea, and my father.
HELENA   And Hippolyta.
LYSANDER And he did bid us follow to the temple.
DEMETRIUS Why, then, we are awake. Let's follow him,   195
    And by the way let us recount our dreams.

Exeunt lovers

Bottom wakes.

BOTTOM When my cue comes, call me, and I will answer. My next is
'Most fair Pyramus'. Heigh ho! Peter Quince? Flute the bellows-
mender? Snout the tinker? Starveling? God's my life! Stolen hence
and left me asleep! I have had a most rare vision. I have had a dream,   200
past the wit of man to say what dream it was. Man is but an ass
if he go about to expound this dream. Methought I was – there is
no man can tell what. Methought I was – and methought I had – but
man is but a patched fool if he will offer to say what methought
I had. The eye of man hath not heard, the ear of man hath not seen,   205
man's hand is not able to taste, his tongue to conceive, nor his heart
to report what my dream was! I will get Peter Quince to write a
ballad of this dream; it shall be called 'Bottom's Dream', because
it hath no bottom; and I will sing it in the latter end of a play, before
the Duke. Peradventure, to make it the more gracious, I shall sing   210
it at her death.   *Exit*

The Mechanicals, without Bottom, despair (they had been looking forward to a regular salary from the duke for their performance). But Bottom suddenly arrives with the news that their play has been chosen.

1 The Mechanicals: a team? (in groups of six)

Take parts and read the whole scene opposite. Then talk together about what sort of relationship the Mechanicals seem to have at this moment. Compare your impression with the picture above and those on other pages. Do the Mechanicals seem a team that works well together? Use evidence from the play to justify your views.

transported carried away
discharge perform
paramour ... thing of naught a
  mistress and, to Flute,
  something immoral and
  wicked

made men our fortunes would be
  made
pumps shoes
presently immediately
preferred recommended for
  performance

Act 4 Scene 2
Athens

Enter QUINCE, FLUTE, SNOUT *and* STARVELING.

QUINCE Have you sent to Bottom's house? Is he come home yet?

STARVELING He cannot be heard of. Out of doubt he is transported.

FLUTE If he come not, then the play is marred. It goes not forward.
   Doth it?

QUINCE It is not possible. You have not a man in all Athens able to   5
   discharge Pyramus but he.

FLUTE No, he hath simply the best wit of any handicraft man in Athens.

QUINCE Yea, and the best person, too; and he is a very paramour for
   a sweet voice.

FLUTE You must say 'paragon'. A paramour is (God bless us!) a thing   10
   of naught.   *Enter* SNUG *the joiner.*

SNUG Masters, the Duke is coming from the temple, and there is two
   or three lords and ladies more married. If our sport had gone
   forward, we had all been made men.

FLUTE O, sweet bully Bottom! Thus hath he lost sixpence a day during   15
   his life: he could not have 'scaped sixpence a day. And the Duke
   had not given him sixpence a day for playing Pyramus, I'll be
   hanged. He would have deserved it. Sixpence a day in Pyramus,
   or nothing.   *Enter* BOTTOM.

BOTTOM Where are these lads? Where are these hearts?   20

QUINCE Bottom! O most courageous day! O most happy hour!

BOTTOM Masters, I am to discourse wonders – but ask me not what;
   for if I tell you, I am not true Athenian. I will tell you everything,
   right as it fell out.

QUINCE Let us hear, sweet Bottom.   25

BOTTOM Not a word of me. All that I will tell you is – that the Duke
   hath dined. Get your apparel together, good strings to your beards,
   new ribbons to your pumps: meet presently at the palace, every man
   look o'er his part. For the short and the long is, our play is preferred.
   In any case, let Thisbe have clean linen; and let not him that plays   30
   the lion pare his nails, for they shall hang out for the lion's claws.
   And, most dear actors, eat no onions nor garlic; for we are to utter
   sweet breath, and I do not doubt but to hear them say it is a sweet
   comedy. No more words. Away! Go, away!   *Exeunt*

Looking back at Act 4
Activities for groups or individuals

1 All conflict ended

In most plays, conflicts are not resolved until the final scene. But *A Midsummer Night's Dream* is different. The play's conflicts are ended, but there is still one more act to come. Only Egeus remains unsatisfied, and he does not appear again. This is a good moment to list what conflicts the play has explored. Write them down and add a paragraph or two on each, analysing its nature, the language used to describe it, and how it was resolved.

2 Titania and Hippolyta: power – and 'doubling'

You could think of both Titania and Hippolyta as 'vanquished' women who have to learn their 'duty' to their lord. But many productions use all kinds of stage business to show that they are not without power and influence (e.g. turn back to p. 110). Remind yourself of all their appearances in the play so far, and write notes on how the language Shakespeare gives them, and the non-verbal techniques an actor can use, show them to have independence of spirit and action.

Also consider the dramatic effect when the two roles are played by the same actor (which quite often occurs in modern productions). List the dramatic advantages and disadvantages of such 'doubling'.

3 Exploring Shakespeare's imagination

Shakespeare has presented a complex 'dream world' which raises many questions. Here are some to start your discussion. What does each group of characters believe about this dream world? What do you make of it? Whose imagination is at work here: the characters', Shakespeare's, the audience's? What do you think Shakespeare might have had in mind when he created *A Midsummer Night's Dream*?

4 A fifty-word summary

Write an account of what happens in Act 4 in exactly fifty words.

5 Celebrity stories

The gossip columns and celebrity magazines would be having a field day with the prospect of so many weddings to come. Write a few magazine or newspaper gossip stories based on the events of the play up to the end of Act 4. Think about the key questions: What kind of background details would journalists be interested in? From whom would they want a quote? Have they got wind of the strange night in the woods?

How about a *Hello!* or *National Enquirer* type scoop on the weddings to come? Speculate on the scandal, the quotes, the expense of it all, the dress designers . . .

6 One of the Mechanicals at home

Step into role as one of the Mechanicals. When you arrive home, you tell your family your story: the rehearsal in the woods, the play, your comrades, the confusions, your feelings and so on.

7 Fairies – an assignment

This is what an actor who played a fairy in *A Midsummer Night's Dream* once said: 'The minute you say "fairy" to people, they think they know exactly what it is.'

Prepare an assignment on fairies. It can include notes, different kinds of illustrations, extracts from the play and so on. To get started, look at the many pictures of fairies throughout this edition. Also consider the fairies' names, and think of what they do in the play. Then think about the possibilities:

- Fairies at the bottom of the garden. The film *Fairy Tale* is a brilliant example of this (it is based on the true story of two young girls who claimed to see and photograph real fairies).
- Non-human spirits.
- A way of bringing on stage the world of fantasy and imagination.
- Representatives of magical and spiritual forces in human lives.

8 Stage the weddings

Shakespeare does not show the actual marriage ceremonies. Write the missing scene yourself – and act it out.

Theseus and Hippolyta talk about the lovers' story, and the power of imagination in poet, lover and madman – who all see things that are not there.

---

1 Imaginations: poets', lunatics' and lovers' (in pairs)

The final scene opens with Theseus and Hippolyta discussing the strange events. To gain a first impression, take roles and speak lines 1–27. Then talk together about the following questions.

a Theseus speaks of the imagination of different kinds of people, including 'the poet'. Remind yourselves of the description of what the poet does (lines 12–17). How far does it describe *A Midsummer Night's Dream* itself?

b Perhaps lines 12–17 are a tongue-in-cheek reference to the work of playwrights. Is Shakespeare cautioning you not to take his work too seriously? Do you? What do you think Shakespeare would have to say about his play being set for examinations?

c What part do the imaginations of 'lovers' and 'lunatics' have in the play?

2 'Drama' and 'poetry' (in pairs)

Shakespeare was a playwright, and he was also a poet of genius. The speeches of Theseus and Titania are considered to be among the finest examples of Shakespeare's dramatic poetry. Sometimes actors are criticised for speaking the speeches opposite simply as poetry, rather than as part of the dramatic script of a play.

Talk together about what you consider to be the differences between 'poetry' and 'dramatic poetry'. Pool your ideas on how the actors could deliver the lines to ensure that the audience experiences both 'poetry' and 'drama'. Put your ideas into practice by performing the lines.

---

toys tales
seething agitated
compact composed

Helen Helen of Troy (a famous beauty)
bodies forth creates
constancy certainty

Act 5 Scene 1
Athens Theseus' Palace

Enter THESEUS, HIPPOLYTA, PHILOSTRATE, Lords and
Attendants.

HIPPOLYTA 'Tis strange, my Theseus, that these lovers speak of.
THESEUS More strange than true. I never may believe
These antique fables, nor these fairy toys.
Lovers and madmen have such seething brains,
Such shaping fantasies, that apprehend   5
More than cool reason ever comprehends.
The lunatic, the lover, and the poet
Are of imagination all compact:
One sees more devils than vast hell can hold;
That is the madman. The lover, all as frantic,   10
Sees Helen's beauty in a brow of Egypt.
The poet's eye, in a fine frenzy rolling,
Doth glance from heaven to earth, from earth to heaven;
And as imagination bodies forth
The forms of things unknown, the poet's pen   15
Turns them to shapes, and gives to airy nothing
A local habitation and a name.
Such tricks hath strong imagination
That if it would but apprehend some joy,
It comprehends some bringer of that joy;   20
Or in the night, imagining some fear,
How easy is a bush supposed a bear?
HIPPOLYTA But all the story of the night told over,
And all their minds transfigured so together,
More witnesseth than fancy's images,   25
And grows to something of great constancy;
But howsoever, strange and admirable.

The lovers enter, and Theseus looks through the list of performances ready for the evening's entertainment. He rejects the first three, but is attracted by the play of Pyramus and Thisbe.

The stage audience: the lovers wait for the entertainment.

masques dances or entertainments where masks were worn
abridgement pastime, making time go quickly
beguile cheat
brief a summary
eunuch castrated man
tipsy Bacchanals drunken women (from Greek mythology)
Thracian from Greece
device entertainment
Muses goddesses of learning and art
satire ridicule
Not sorting with not appropriate to
concord harmony

Enter the lovers: LYSANDER, DEMETRIUS, HERMIA *and* HELENA.

THESEUS Here come the lovers, full of joy and mirth.
     Joy, gentle friends, joy and fresh days of love
     Accompany your hearts!
LYSANDER   More than to us   30
     Wait in your royal walks, your board, your bed!
THESEUS Come now: what masques, what dances shall we have
     To wear away this long age of three hours
     Between our after-supper and bedtime?
     Where is our usual manager of mirth?   35
     What revels are in hand? Is there no play
     To ease the anguish of a torturing hour?
     Call Philostrate.
PHILOSTRATE   Here, mighty Theseus.
THESEUS Say, what abridgement have you for this evening?
     What masque, what music? How shall we beguile   40
     The lazy time if not with some delight?
PHILOSTRATE [*Giving him a paper.*]
     There is a brief how many sports are ripe.
     Make choice of which your highness will see first.
THESEUS [*Reading.*]
     'The battle with the Centaurs, to be sung
     By an Athenian eunuch to the harp' –   45
     We'll none of that; that have I told my love
     In glory of my kinsman, Hercules.
     [*Reading.*] 'The riot of the tipsy Bacchanals,
     Tearing the Thracian singer in their rage' –
     That is an old device, and it was played   50
     When I from Thebes came last a conqueror.
     [*Reading.*] 'The thrice three Muses mourning for the death
     Of learning, late deceased in beggary' –
     That is some satire keen and critical,
     Not sorting with a nuptial ceremony.   55
     [*Reading.*] 'A tedious brief scene of young Pyramus
     And his love Thisbe, very tragical mirth' –
     Merry and tragical? Tedious and brief?
     That is hot ice and wondrous strange snow!
     How shall we find the concord of this discord?   60

Theseus decides on the Mechanicals' play despite the objections of
Philostrate, who says the rehearsal was laughably bad.

1 Philostrate – a snob? (in pairs)

Philostrate tries to convince Theseus that the Mechanicals' play is
not worth seeing. Take turns to catch his superior tone of voice,
pinching your nose between your thumb and fingers as you speak all
he says opposite. Afterwards, talk together about whether he is being
fair to the Mechanicals, and whether he is worried as much by their
social class as by the quality of their performance.

2 Two audiences – two responses (in pairs)

The Mechanicals will perform to two audiences: the court, and the
theatre audience. The theatre audience gets an outsider's view of the
Mechanicals' play in Philostrate's description (lines 61–70).

a Suggest reasons why Shakespeare included Philostrate's
  description of the play (after all, both audiences are about to see
  it). Discuss whether you think that both audiences will react in
  the same way (you will discover the views of the onstage
  audience very shortly).

b Think of other plays, films and TV shows which 'layer' your
  responses (that is, respond to the performance *and* to the onstage
  audience's response). Examples are *Hamlet*, the film *The Truman
  Show*, and the TV *Jerry Springer Show*. Discuss the dramatic
  effect of such stagings.

3 Hippolyta's response: 'I love not to see . . . '

How might Hippolyta speak lines 85–6? Suggest what they reveal
about her (and as you read on compare her words to the men's
responses).

---

toiled work until weary
unbreathed unpractised
sport fun, entertainment
conned learnt

wretchedness o'ercharged those of
little ability overstretched (or poor
people made mock of)

PHILOSTRATE A play there is, my lord, some ten words long,
     Which is as 'brief' as I have known a play,
     But by ten words, my lord, it is too long,
     Which makes it 'tedious'. For in all the play
     There is not one word apt, one player fitted.   65
     And 'tragical', my noble lord, it is,
     For Pyramus therein doth kill himself,
     Which when I saw rehearsed, I must confess,
     Made mine eyes water; but more 'merry' tears
     The passion of loud laughter never shed.   70
THESEUS What are they that do play it?
PHILOSTRATE Hard-handed men that work in Athens here,
     Which never laboured in their minds till now;
     And now have toiled their unbreathed memories
     With this same play against your nuptial.   75
THESEUS And we will hear it.
PHILOSTRATE   No, my noble lord,
     It is not for you. I have heard it over,
     And it is nothing, nothing in the world,
     Unless you can find sport in their intents,
     Extremely stretched, and conned with cruel pain,   80
     To do you service.
THESEUS   I will hear that play;
     For never anything can be amiss
     When simpleness and duty tender it.
     Go bring them in; and take your places, ladies.
                              [*Exit Philostrate*]
HIPPOLYTA I love not to see wretchedness o'ercharged,   85
     And duty in his service perishing.
THESEUS Why, gentle sweet, you shall see no such thing.
HIPPOLYTA He says they can do nothing in this kind.

Theseus explains his choice of the Mechanicals' play: it is the thought that counts among simple people. Quince then enters and begins the play, rather strangely.

---

1 On show – does it make you tongue-tied? (in small groups)

We are all on show to others every time we are in public. But great occasions can stop us speaking altogether. In lines 93–105 Theseus talks about learned people such as 'great clerks' being unable to talk during official welcomes. He also criticises the 'audacious eloquence' of those who speak a little too well in public. Theseus prefers 'love' (in the sense of sincere affection) and 'tongue-tied simplicity': those who speak little ('least') communicate a great deal ('speak most'). Describe occasions when you personally have had to speak in public or to a high-status person and have found it intimidating (e.g. in the classroom, or in an assembly or on stage).

2 Watch your punctuation! (in pairs)

Quince's Prologue (lines 108–17) has much of its punctuation in the wrong place (that's why the court jokes about his 'points' and 'stops' – the punctuation). One person speaks the speech as it is written. The other repunctuates and speaks it to make better sense. Which version works best dramatically? Why?

3 Asides: does Quince hear? (in groups of four)

Discuss whether Quince hears the comments of the court (lines 118–23), or whether they are Asides (heard only by the audience). Try acting it out both ways: if Quince hears, he will react; if he doesn't, he simply carries on. Remember, 'dramatic effect' is your guide: what the audience most enjoys. Keep this 'overhearing' notion in mind for the rest of the Mechanicals' play.

---

in might, not merit accepts it, given the ability of those that offer it
premeditated welcomes planned speeches
periods stops
capacity understanding

addressed ready
stand upon points take notice of punctuation or detail
stop a pun on full stop, and suddenly stopping a horse when riding
in government under control

THESEUS The kinder we, to give them thanks for nothing.
      Our sport shall be to take what they mistake;   90
      And what poor duty cannot do, noble respect
      Takes it in might, not merit.
      Where I have come, great clerks have purposèd
      To greet me with premeditated welcomes,
      Where I have seen them shiver and look pale,   95
      Make periods in the midst of sentences,
      Throttle their practised accent in their fears,
      And in conclusion dumbly have broke off,
      Not paying me a welcome. Trust me, sweet,
      Out of this silence yet I picked a welcome,   100
      And in the modesty of fearful duty
      I read as much as from the rattling tongue
      Of saucy and audacious eloquence.
      Love, therefore, and tongue-tied simplicity
      In least speak most, to my capacity.   105

[Enter Philostrate.]

PHILOSTRATE So please your grace, the Prologue is addressed.
THESEUS Let him approach.
               Flourish of trumpets.

Enter QUINCE *as Prologue.*

QUINCE   If we offend, it is with our good will.
        That you should think, we come not to offend,
      But with good will. To show our simple skill,   110
        That is the true beginning of our end.
      Consider then, we come but in despite.
        We do not come as minding to content you,
      Our true intent is. All for your delight,
        We are not here. That you should here repent you, 115
      The actors are at hand; and by their show
      You shall know all that you are like to know.
THESEUS This fellow doth not stand upon points.
LYSANDER He hath rid his prologue like a rough colt; he knows not
    the stop. A good moral, my lord; it is not enough to speak, but to 120
    speak true.
HIPPOLYTA Indeed, he hath played on this prologue like a child on
    a recorder – a sound, but not in government.

Theseus comments on how mixed up Quince's introduction was. Quince continues with the Prologue, which explains the play, and introduces the characters.

1 The Prologue – an outline of the play (in groups of six)

Quince's description of the play the Mechanicals are about to perform is usually a hilarious sequence in the theatre. This is your chance to work on the lines to create a really funny performance. Take parts and work on the following activities.

a **Entrances and exits**   At the beginning of the Prologue, all the Mechanicals come on to the stage and all but Snout exit at the end of it. How would you have them do this? For example, it might be a noisy and messy entrance and exit; or perhaps more subdued, with the Mechanicals overawed by the occasion. The possibilities are endless. Try out a few ideas.

b **Mime to the Prologue**   As Quince speaks the Prologue, each of the Mechanicals comes forward and mimes the character or object they are portraying. Experiment with different ways of presenting your mimes. It may be by acting completely over the top, or stumbling and muddling, or in any other way which you think might work. Is it possible to be funny, foolish, and endearing? Try out ways to achieve that impression.

c **The play itself**   Talk together about what the Prologue suggests about the kind of play the Mechanicals will present. Also discuss the likely dramatic impact of such a description, and what this tells you about the Mechanicals and their ideas about what a play should be.

d **Comparison**   Compare this Prologue (lines 126–50) to Quince's previous introduction to the play in lines 108–17. Think about how they are dramatically different – and why.

---

sunder   keep apart
lanthorn   lantern
hight   is called
mantle   cloak
fall   let fall

Anon   soon
broached   stabbed
tarrying   waiting
twain   two

THESEUS His speech was like a tangled chain, nothing impaired, but all disordered. Who is next?　　　　　　　　　　　125

Enter with a Trumpeter before them [BOTTOM *as*] *Pyramus,*
[FLUTE *as*] *Thisbe,* [SNOUT *as*] *Wall,* [STARVELING *as*]
Moonshine and [SNUG *as*] *Lion.*

QUINCE (*as Prologue*)
　　　Gentles, perchance you wonder at this show,
　　　　　But wonder on, till truth make all things plain.
　　　This man is Pyramus, if you would know;
　　　　　This beauteous lady Thisbe is, certain.
　　　This man with lime and rough-cast doth present　　　130
　　　　　Wall, that vile wall which did these lovers sunder;
　　　And through Wall's chink, poor souls, they are content
　　　　　To whisper – at the which let no man wonder.
　　　This man with lanthorn, dog, and bush of thorn,
　　　　　Presenteth Moonshine; for, if you will know,　　　135
　　　By moonshine did these lovers think no scorn
　　　　　To meet at Ninus' tomb, there, there to woo.
　　　This grisly beast, which Lion hight by name,
　　　The trusty Thisbe, coming first by night,
　　　Did scare away, or rather did affright;　　　140
　　　And as she fled, her mantle she did fall,
　　　　　Which Lion vile with bloody mouth did stain.
　　　Anon comes Pyramus, sweet youth and tall,
　　　　　And finds his trusty Thisbe's mantle slain;
　　　Whereat with blade, with bloody, blameful blade,　　　145
　　　　　He bravely broached his boiling bloody breast;
　　　And Thisbe, tarrying in mulberry shade,
　　　　　His dagger drew, and died. For all the rest,
　　　Let Lion, Moonshine, Wall, and lovers twain
　　　At large discourse, while here they do remain.　　　150
　　　　　Exeunt Quince, Bottom, Flute, Snug and Starveling

Snout, as the Wall, explains his role. Bottom, as Pyramus, enters and begins the play's action.

---

1 Snout's opportunity – Wall! (in pairs)

Snout gets his great opportunity to speak as Wall. After his speech opposite, he has only two more lines in the play, so he will surely make the most of lines 153–62. Take turns to step into role and deliver his speech. Make the most of the rhymes and the stage directions that are built in to the language. Later, when you have time, you could design and make his costume, but for the moment concentrate on how to speak and act.

2 Bottom's up! (in pairs)

At last Bottom gets his chance to show what he can do. And in every production of the play he seizes it whole-heartedly and throws himself into the role of tragic hero. Here's a chance to be Bottom, so take turns acting out his first speech (lines 167–78) – your partner can be the admiring Wall. Bottom's speech is full of repetitions of words, sounds and ideas, so use them to increase the comedy. Here are some hints:

'O'   Bottom's notion of a tragic hero is that he uses 'O' whenever he can – so make the most of those exclamations.

Rhymes   There are all kinds of rhymes in the speech, not simply at the ends of lines. Exploit them for comic effect.

Rhythms   The lines are very rhythmical: phrases or sentences echo each other. Bottom thinks he must do full justice to those rhythms, making sure his audience really hears them.

Words   Bottom wants to convince his audience that it is 'night', that he speaks to 'Wall', and that he's sad ('alack'). Emphasise!

---

interlude   short play
sinister   left
partition   wall (or section of a speech)

curse again   should curse back, since it is 'sensible' (alive)
fall pat   come right

THESEUS I wonder if the lion be to speak?

DEMETRIUS No wonder, my lord; one lion may, when many asses do.

SNOUT (*as Wall*)

    In this same interlude it doth befall

    That I, one Snout by name, present a wall;

    And such a wall as I would have you think   155

    That had in it a crannied hole or chink,

    Through which the lovers, Pyramus and Thisbe,

    Did whisper often, very secretly.

    This loam, this rough-cast, and this stone doth show

    That I am that same wall; the truth is so.   160

    And this the cranny is, right and sinister,

    Through which the fearful lovers are to whisper.

THESEUS Would you desire lime and hair to speak better?

DEMETRIUS It is the wittiest partition that ever I heard discourse, my

    lord.   165

Enter [Bottom as] Pyramus.

THESEUS Pyramus draws near the wall; silence!

BOTTOM (*as Pyramus*)

    O grim-looked night, O night with hue so black,

      O night which ever art when day is not!

    O night, O night, alack, alack, alack,

      I fear my Thisbe's promise is forgot!   170

    And thou, O wall, O sweet, O lovely wall,

      That stand'st between her father's ground and mine,

    Thou wall, O wall, O sweet and lovely wall,

      Show me thy chink, to blink through with mine eyne.

        [Wall parts his fingers.]

    Thanks, courteous wall; Jove shield thee well for this!   175

      But what see I? No Thisbe do I see.

    O wicked wall, through whom I see no bliss,

      Cursed be thy stones for thus deceiving me!

THESEUS The wall, methinks, being sensible, should curse again.

BOTTOM No, in truth sir, he should not. 'Deceiving me' is Thisbe's   180

    cue. She is to enter now, and I am to spy her through the wall.

    You shall see it will fall pat as I told you. Yonder she comes.

Thisbe and Pyramus declare their love for each other through the chink in the wall, and agree to meet at 'Ninny's tomb'.

1 Gooseberry (in groups of three)

Snout, as Wall, is the gooseberry or overhearer, so he has an important part to play as he reacts to what he hears. Talk together about his possible responses, then discuss Flute's adopted 'female' voice and actions. Finally, get up and act the lines in different ways.

Limander, Helen (these should be Leander and Hero, two legendary lovers)
Fates see page 136

Shafalus, Procrus (these should be Cephalus and Procris, more legendary lovers)
Tide come

Enter [Flute as] Thisbe.

FLUTE (*as Thisbe*)
    O wall, full often hast thou heard my moans,
        For parting my fair Pyramus and me.
    My cherry lips have often kissed thy stones,   185
        Thy stones with lime and hair knit up in thee.
BOTTOM (*as Pyramus*)
    I see a voice; now will I to the chink,
        To spy and I can hear my Thisbe's face.
    Thisbe!
FLUTE (*as Thisbe*)
            My love! Thou art my love, I think?
BOTTOM (*as Pyramus*)
    Think what thou wilt, I am thy lover's grace,   190
    And like Limander am I trusty still.
FLUTE (*as Thisbe*)
    And I like Helen, till the Fates me kill.
BOTTOM (*as Pyramus*)
    Not Shafalus to Procrus was so true.
FLUTE (*as Thisbe*)
    As Shafalus to Procrus, I to you.
BOTTOM (*as Pyramus*)
    O, kiss me through the hole of this vile wall!   195
FLUTE (*as Thisbe*)
    I kiss the wall's hole, not your lips at all.
BOTTOM (*as Pyramus*)
    Wilt thou at Ninny's tomb meet me straightway?
FLUTE (*as Thisbe*)
    Tide life, tide death, I come without delay.
                [Exeunt Bottom and Flute in different directions]

The stage audience comments on the play, and Snug (the lion) enters, explaining he is not really a lion.

1 A silly ridiculous play? Or . . .? (in small groups)

Hippolyta says, 'This is the silliest stuff that ever I heard.' Her comment echoes what Samuel Pepys said when he saw the play in 1662: 'We saw *Midsummer Night's Dreame*, which I have never seen before, nor shall ever again, for it is the most insipid ridiculous play that I ever saw in my life.' Theseus replies to Hippolyta, 'The best in this kind are but shadows'.

Talk together about the following three questions. What are your responses to Hippolyta's and Pepys's views? What might Shakespeare have replied to Pepys if he had the chance? What are possible meanings of Theseus's remark?

---

mural wall
wilful ready
fell fierce
dam mother (lioness)

fox . . . goose the lion was supposed to be brave, the fox cunning (with 'discretion') and the goose stupid

SNOUT (*as Wall*)

> Thus have I, Wall, my part dischargèd so;
>
> And being done, thus Wall away doth go.   *Exit*   200

THESEUS Now is the mural down between the two neighbours.

DEMETRIUS No remedy, my lord, when walls are so wilful to hear
without warning.

HIPPOLYTA This is the silliest stuff that ever I heard.

THESEUS The best in this kind are but shadows; and the worst are no   205
worse, if imagination amend them.

HIPPOLYTA It must be your imagination then, and not theirs.

THESEUS If we imagine no worse of them than they of themselves, they
may pass for excellent men. Here come two noble beasts in, a man
and a lion.   210

> *Enter [Snug as] Lion and [Starveling as] Moonshine.*

SNUG (*as Lion*)

> You ladies, you whose gentle hearts do fear
>
> > The smallest monstrous mouse that creeps on floor,
>
> May now, perchance, both quake and tremble here,
>
> > When Lion rough in wildest rage doth roar.
>
> Then know that I as Snug the joiner am   215
>
> A lion fell, nor else no lion's dam;
>
> For if I should as lion come in strife
>
> Into this place, 'twere pity on my life.

THESEUS A very gentle beast, and of a good conscience.

DEMETRIUS The very best at a beast, my lord, that e'er I saw.   220

LYSANDER This lion is a very fox for his valour.

THESEUS True; and a goose for his discretion.

DEMETRIUS Not so, my lord; for his valour cannot carry his discretion;
and the fox carries the goose.

THESEUS His discretion, I am sure, cannot carry his valour; for the   225
goose carries not the fox. It is well: leave it to his discretion, and
let us listen to the moon.

Starveling, as the Moon, manages to explain his role, despite the comments of the stage audience. Thisbe arrives, only to be frightened away by the lion.

1 An unruly – and snobbish – audience? (in groups of seven)

The stage audience seems to be getting out of hand. Starveling finds his performance is not appreciated. Take parts and read through lines 228–55 several times. Consider how Starveling says his lines 242–4. Is he irritated with the audience, intimidated by them, bored with the whole thing? Flute and Snug get a similar mocking response as the audience shouts out ironic comments like a football crowd. After your readings talk together about the following.

a Why (and how) does Starveling seem to give up speaking his lines?

b The comments made about the players and the play show the attitude the court has to the Mechanicals' play. What social-class issues could be raised through the way in which those remarks are spoken?

c Might the Mechanicals feel superior to their audience, just as their audience feels superior to them? To explore this, you could suggest how the lovers might have presented the story of Pyramus and Thisbe – and how the Mechanicals would respond to *their* performance.

2 Imagining the moon (in small groups)

The image of the moon is common throughout *A Midsummer Night's Dream*. Find some earlier references to the moon and compare them with the presentation of the moon opposite. Using those earlier quotations, discuss the differences between what the audience are asked to do in the whole play (imagine both the moon and its effects just from Shakespeare's words) and what the Mechanicals think their audience needs.

---

horns on his head   the sign of a cuckold (someone whose wife has been unfaithful)
crescent   waxing moon (growing larger)

already in snuff   already snuffed out
Well moused   (the lion is like a cat with a mouse – the mantle)

STARVELING (*as Moonshine*)
>This lanthorn doth the hornèd moon present –

DEMETRIUS He should have worn the horns on his head.

THESEUS He is no crescent, and his horns are invisible within the   230
circumference.

STARVELING (*as Moonshine*)
>This lanthorn doth the hornèd moon present;
>
>>Myself the man i'th'moon do seem to be –

THESEUS This is the greatest error of all the rest; the man should be
put into the lantern. How is it else the man i'th'moon?   235

DEMETRIUS He dares not come there, for the candle; for you see it is
already in snuff.

HIPPOLYTA I am aweary of this moon. Would he would change!

THESEUS It appears by his small light of discretion that he is in the
wane; but yet in courtesy, in all reason, we must stay the time.   240

LYSANDER Proceed, Moon.

STARVELING All that I have to say is to tell you that the lanthorn is
the moon, I the man i'th'moon, this thorn bush my thorn bush
and this dog my dog.

DEMETRIUS Why, all these should be in the lantern, for all these are   245
in the moon. But silence: here comes Thisbe.

Enter [Flute as] Thisbe.

FLUTE (*as Thisbe*)
>This is old Ninny's tomb. Where is my love?

SNUG (*as Lion*) O!

>*Lion roars. Thisbe runs off [dropping her mantle]*

DEMETRIUS Well roared, Lion!

THESEUS Well run, Thisbe!   250

HIPPOLYTA Well shone, Moon! Truly, the moon shines with a good
grace.

THESEUS Well moused, Lion!

DEMETRIUS And then came Pyramus –

LYSANDER And so the lion vanished.   255

>*[Lion worries Thisbe's mantle, and exit]*

Pyramus enters full of expectation. He then sees Thisbe's blood-stained mantle, and calls for his own death.

1 Bottom struts his stuff (in small groups)

Now Bottom really gets the chance to display his acting skills. His speech opposite and his lines 275–90 on the next page are all part of the same sequence. First get some experience of his whole performance by taking turns to speak as Bottom from line 256 to 290. Use the suggestions in Activity 2 on page 128 (on repetitions) and below to help you make the episode as funny as possible.

a **Humour**   Shakespeare makes Bottom's attempts at acting humorous partly through Bottom's overuse of alliteration: 'gracious, golden, glittering gleams'. Make sure he emphasises all those hard 'g's.

b **Iambic pentameter** (see p. 165)   Bottom begins with four lines in the traditional style of tragic heroes: lines with five beats. He will make sure that his audience appreciates that he knows his classics. Ensure that five emphatic stresses come over in each line. You will find he does just the same in his next speech, on page 139.

c **Doggerel**   Bottom does not keep up the 'high style' of his beginning. He changes to the very simple rhythms of two or three beats to a line. Again, take every opportunity to bring out those rhythms.

2 Romeo and Juliet – a parody?

As you work on the Mechanicals' play, keep thinking about whether Shakespeare is mocking his own *Romeo and Juliet*, which he wrote around the same time as *A Midsummer Night's Dream*. Watch for similarities.

---

dole   reason for sadness
Furies   avenging goddesses
Fates . . . thread and thrum   the goddesses controlling lives, spinning out the threads of people's lives, and ending them by cutting the thread and thrum (tuft on a thread)

Quail   destroy
quell   kill
Beshrew my heart   (exclamation, like 'Bless my soul')

Enter [Bottom as] Pyramus.

BOTTOM (*as Pyramus*)
>Sweet moon, I thank thee for thy sunny beams;
>>I thank thee, moon, for shining now so bright;
>For by thy gracious, golden, glittering gleams
>>I trust to take of truest Thisbe sight.
>>>But stay – O spite!   260
>>>But mark, poor Knight,
>>What dreadful dole is here?
>>>Eyes, do you see?
>>>How can it be?
>>O dainty duck, O dear!   265
>>>Thy mantle good –
>>>What, stained with blood?
>>Approach, ye Furies fell!
>>>O Fates, come, come,
>>>Cut thread and thrum,   270
>>Quail, crush, conclude, and quell.

THESEUS This passion, and the death of a dear friend, would go near
to make a man look sad.

HIPPOLYTA Beshrew my heart, but I pity the man.

Pyramus stabs himself, and has a prolonged death. As the audience comments on the acting, Thisbe enters.

---

1 Bottom's great moment (in small groups)

There are helpful suggestions on Bottom's final speech on page 136. Remind yourself of them, and speak Pyramus's death scene opposite. On stage, Bottom often mistakes right for left as he searches for his heart. He usually takes a very long time to deliver his final line, milking every 'die' for laughs. Follow his example.

2 *Enter* THISBE – a good-looking girl?

Look at the man playing Flute (Thisbe) in the photograph on page 140. Think about whether you like the image he puts across, and what Flute might be like if played by very different-looking actors. The actor on page 130, for example, looks much more feminine.

3 An ass by any other name? (in small groups)

Yet again, someone implies that Bottom is an 'ass' (line 294). With a name like Bottom, and having an ass's head at one point, this idea of his character is pretty clear. Think about what Bottom says and does throughout the play, and make a list of reasons why Bottom is – or isn't – an ass. Find quotes for and against.

4 *Shakespeare in Love*: the film

The film *Shakespeare in Love* deals very creatively with the concept of women on the stage in Elizabethan England. The film provides an enjoyable background to the study of Shakespeare's plays. If you have seen it, write a paragraph on what it adds to your understanding of *A Midsummer Night's Dream*.

---

deflowered wasted
pap breast
die (line 291) one of a pair of dice; ace (one) is the lowest throw (Demetrius puns on Bottom's use of 'die')

mote tiny particle
balance scale
means, videlicet moans, makes a formal legal complaint

BOTTOM (*as Pyramus*)

      O wherefore, Nature, didst thou lions frame,   275

          Since lion vile hath here deflowered my dear?

      Which is – no, no – which was the fairest dame

          That lived, that loved, that liked, that looked with cheer.

               Come tears, confound!

               Out sword, and wound   280

            The pap of Pyramus,

              Ay, that left pap,

            Where heart doth hop:

           Thus die I, thus, thus, thus! [*Stabs himself.*]

            Now am I dead,   285

            Now am I fled;

          My soul is in the sky.

             Tongue, lose thy light;

             Moon, take thy flight;

                                     [*Exit Starveling*]

          Now die, die, die, die, die. [*He dies.*]   290

DEMETRIUS No die, but an ace for him; for he is but one.

LYSANDER Less than an ace, man; for he is dead, he is nothing.

THESEUS With the help of a surgeon he might yet recover, and yet prove
an ass.

HIPPOLYTA How chance Moonshine is gone before Thisbe comes back   295
and finds her lover?

THESEUS She will find him by starlight.

Enter [Flute as] Thisbe.

Here she comes and her passion ends the play.

HIPPOLYTA Methinks she should not use a long one for such a
Pyramus; I hope she will be brief.   300

DEMETRIUS A mote will turn the balance, which Pyramus, which
Thisbe is the better: he for a man, God warrant us; she for a woman,
God bless us.

LYSANDER She hath spied him already, with those sweet eyes.

DEMETRIUS And thus she means, videlicet –   305

Thisbe realises Pyramus is dead and kills herself. Bottom asks if the duke wants an epilogue or a dance. Theseus settles on the country dance.

Compare and contrast the death scene of Pyramus with that of Thisbe. Consider how visuals like costume, props and facial expressions can be used to heighten humour. How much sadness or pathos would you like to convey? Discuss how the characters of Bottom and Flute can be developed through how they perform as the doomed lovers.

1 'Your play needs no excuse' (in small groups)

Discuss whether the Mechanicals' play needs excusing (line 335), and then look again at the plays Theseus had a choice of viewing (lines 44–60). Decide whether Theseus's choice was wise, bearing in mind how the audience reacted to the Mechanicals' play. Report back to the rest of the class with your conclusions.

---

sisters three   the Fates (see the gloss on p. 136)
gore   blood
shore   cut
thread of silk   life-line

imbrue   stab, make bloody
notably discharged   admirably performed
Bergomask   a country dance

FLUTE (*as Thisbe*)
    Asleep, my love?
    What, dead, my dove?
  O Pyramus, arise.
    Speak, speak! Quite dumb?
    Dead, dead? A tomb 310
  Must cover thy sweet eyes.
    These lily lips,
    This cherry nose,
  These yellow cowslip cheeks
    Are gone, are gone. 315
    Lovers, make moan;
  His eyes were green as leeks.
    O sisters three,
    Come, come to me
  With hands as pale as milk; 320
    Lay them in gore,
    Since you have shore
  With shears his thread of silk.
    Tongue, not a word!
    Come, trusty sword, 325
  Come blade, my breast imbrue! [*Stabs herself.*]
    And farewell, friends.
    Thus Thisbe ends –
  Adieu, adieu, adieu! [*Dies.*]

THESEUS Moonshine and Lion are left to bury the dead. 330

DEMETRIUS Ay, and Wall, too.

BOTTOM [*Starting up, as Flute does also.*] No, I assure you, the wall is down that parted their fathers. Will it please you to see the epilogue, or to hear a Bergomask dance between two of our company?

THESEUS No epilogue, I pray you; for your play needs no excuse. Never 335 excuse; for when the players are all dead, there need none to be blamed. Marry, if he that writ it had played Pyramus and hanged himself in Thisbe's garter, it would have been a fine tragedy: and so it is, truly, and very notably discharged. But come, your Bergomask; let your epilogue alone. 340

The Mechanicals dance, the duke instructs everyone to go to bed, and Puck enters. He speaks of the night, the time when the fairies play.

---

1 What kind of dance? (in groups of four)

It was common in Shakespeare's day for plays to end with a dance. The Bergomask was a country dance. Would you want to continue with the physical humour of their play or would you want to give them some quiet dignity in their final scene?

2 Puck's night-time world (whole class)

Listen as your teacher reads Puck's speech (lines 349–68) aloud several times. Draw what you consider to be the major night-time images. Share your final design with a partner. Have you picked up the same images or focused on different ones? Describe the mood presented by your images. The results might make a classroom display.

3 Two speeches – two moods? (in pairs)

One person read Theseus's speech, the other Puck's. Think carefully about differences between them, particularly in mood and images. Read the two speeches again, this time with actions, trying to emphasise those differences between them (you may find some similarities). If you were directing the play, what lighting effects would you use during lines 348–9?

4 Three worlds – three accounts (in groups of three)

The mortals have left, and the fairy world begins its entrance. Choose one lover, one of the Mechanicals and one member of the court and write a diary account of the evening. Concentrate on perceptions, thoughts and feelings rather than simply describing events.

---

iron tongue . . . told   the bell was struck
overwatched   watched over
palpable-gross   obviously uncouth
heavy gait   laboured passage, slow-moving pace

heavy (line 351)   tired
foredone   worn out
wasted brands   burnt logs
triple Hecate's team   the moon's chariot
hallowed   saintly

[The company return; two of them dance, then exeunt Bottom, Flute and their fellows.]

The iron tongue of midnight hath told twelve.
Lovers, to bed; 'tis almost fairy time.
I fear we shall outsleep the coming morn
As much as we this night have overwatched.
This palpable-gross play hath well beguiled   345
The heavy gait of night. Sweet friends, to bed.
A fortnight hold we this solemnity
In nightly revels and new jollity.

Exeunt

Enter PUCK *[carrying a broom].*

PUCK   Now the hungry lion roars,
        And the wolf behowls the moon,   350
Whilst the heavy ploughman snores,
        All with weary task foredone.
Now the wasted brands do glow,
        Whilst the screech-owl, screeching loud,
Puts the wretch that lies in woe   355
        In remembrance of a shroud.
Now it is the time of night
        That the graves, all gaping wide,
Every one lets forth his sprite
        In the church-way paths to glide.   360
And we fairies, that do run
        By the triple Hecate's team
From the presence of the sun,
        Following darkness like a dream,
Now are frolic; not a mouse   365
Shall disturb this hallowed house.
I am sent with broom before
To sweep the dust behind the door.

Oberon and Titania, with their fairies, enter, and Oberon instructs them to go through the house, blessing the three couples with loving marriages and 'perfect' children.

1 Blessing mortal marriages

Oberon delivers the blessing of the fairy world on the three marriages (lines 379–98). He speaks in four-beat rhythm, quite different from the verse of the court and the prose of the Mechanicals. His blessing draws on country myths and folk tales. Speak his lines several times, then write a modern blessing for newly married couples in the manner of lines 379–98. Every culture has its own blessings, and you may wish to draw upon those, but the following blessing on marriage and children from *The Book of Common Prayer* (1662) may help:

> We beseech thee, assist with thy blessing these two persons, that they may both be fruitful in procreation of children, and also live together so long in godly love and honesty, that they may see their children christianly and virtuously brought up, to thy praise and honour; through Jesus Christ our Lord.

2 The fairies' dance (in groups of six or more)

Picking your own music, improvise and develop a dance (and song) to suit the fairies at this moment in the play.

3 From conflict to 'sweet peace' (in small groups)

Compare the speeches opposite with the conflicts of the opening scene and the conflicts in the wood. List the differences. The play dramatises problems in the relationships between women and men. What has brought them to 'sweet peace' now? For each couple, suggest explanations of how their conflicts have been resolved. Think about the spiritual or mental changes, as well as the way the plot works.

---

best bride-bed the wedding bed of Theseus and Hippolyta
issue children

mark prodigious birthmark with an evil omen
take his gait go his way

Enter [OBERON *and* TITANIA,] *the King and Queen of Fairies, with all their train.*

OBERON	Through the house give glimmering light
	By the dead and drowsy fire;
	Every elf and fairy sprite
	Hop as light as bird from briar,
	And this ditty after me
	Sing, and dance it trippingly.
TITANIA	First rehearse your song by rote,
	To each word a warbling note;
	Hand in hand with fairy grace
	Will we sing and bless this place.

Song [*and dance*].

OBERON	Now until the break of day
	Through this house each fairy stray.
	To the best bride-bed will we,
	Which by us shall blessèd be;
	And the issue there create
	Ever shall be fortunate.
	So shall all the couples three
	Ever true in loving be,
	And the blots of nature's hand
	Shall not in their issue stand.
	Never mole, harelip, nor scar,
	Nor mark prodigious, such as are
	Despisèd in nativity,
	Shall upon their children be.
	With this field-dew consecrate,
	Every fairy take his gait,
	And each several chamber bless
	Through this palace with sweet peace;
	And the owner of it blessed
	Ever shall in safety rest.
	Trip away, make no stay;
	Meet me all by break of day.

Exeunt [*all but Puck*]

370
375
380
385
390
395
400

Puck, on his own now, asks for the audience to think of the play as their dream. He promises improved performances and asks for the audience's approval.

1 Speak it (in small groups)

The best thing to do with Puck's farewell is to speak it. So take turns at delivering the lines to the audience of the rest of your group. Help each other by suggesting different ways of increasing dramatic effect. You might try sharing the lines between you, or speaking some chorally. Present your final version to the class.

2 Who else might speak to the audience?

Puck speaks directly to the audience, who in Shakespeare's time would either hiss ('the serpent's tongue') or clap ('Give me your hands') at the end of plays. Plays often ended with a request to the audience to clap (and not hiss). Is Puck the appropriate character to end the play and ask the audience for their applause? Suggest why Shakespeare gives him the final word, even though he has been so mischievous and negative about humans in the play: 'Lord, what fools these mortals be', 'The shallowest thick-skin of that barren sort'. If you had to choose a different character, who would it be – and why?

3 Plays – and dreams (in small groups)

a The Mechanicals have shown their play. Now *A Midsummer Night's Dream* ends with Shakespeare calling the actors 'shadows' (line 401) and the play itself 'visions' (line 404). Discuss how far you think plays, films and TV dramas are 'visions' and their actors 'shadows'.

b The lovers and Bottom have experienced what they think are dreams. Now Puck suggests the whole play is 'but a dream' for the audience. Whose 'dream' is the play – the audience's, Shakespeare's, the mortals in the play, all of these, or . . . ?

---

mend improve
'scape the serpent's tongue escape the audience hissing (because of a poor performance)

Give me your hands applaud
restore amends (Puck will, in return, make amends)

PUCK [*To the audience*]

        If we shadows have offended,
        Think but this, and all is mended:
        That you have but slumbered here
        While these visions did appear;
        And this weak and idle theme,   405
        No more yielding but a dream,
        Gentles, do not reprehend;
        If you pardon, we will mend.
        And, as I am an honest Puck,
        If we have unearnèd luck   410
        Now to 'scape the serpent's tongue
        We will make amends ere long,
        Else the Puck a liar call.
        So, good night unto you all.
        Give me your hands, if we be friends,   415
        And Robin shall restore amends.   [*Exit*]

Looking back at the play
Activities for groups or individuals

Compare this photograph with other images of Puck in the script. Talk together about what you think are the good and bad points of each. How would you present Puck in your own production of *A Midsummer Night's Dream*?

1 Puck – as symbol

'We cannot possibly deal with Puck as a realistic character.' Say whether or not you agree with this statement, then suggest what issues and themes Shakespeare is exploring through this character or dramatic device. Pool your ideas in a small group in the form of a spider diagram.

2 Important to you – why?

Write down what, for you, are the ten most important quotes in the play. Compare your list with a partner's, giving reasons for your choices.

3 The fairy world

a Even in Shakespeare's day, many people did not believe in fairies. Organise a class debate on 'Ghosts, poltergeists and all things supernatural exist only in the imagination.'

b The fairies in the play may represent a 'magical' or 'spiritual' side of our life, or the power of imagination. How might three types of people react to seeing *A Midsummer Night's Dream* and its fairies: a Mechanicals-type person (a worker), a lover (a teenager in love) and a ruler (a politician)? To explore your answers, improvise a scene in which these three people leave the theatre and are interviewed about the play and what they thought of it.

4 What were Shakespeare's views?

What do you think were Shakespeare's own views about the Mechanicals? You may want to take into account the views of the court audience. You could reflect upon class, culture, education, humour, loyalty, society, patronage, respect, responsibility and so on.

5 Unpleasant moments?

Although this play falls firmly into the comedy category of Shakespearean plays, it has its bleak and unpleasant moments and images. Identify particular moments or incidents in the play that you think could be seen as disturbing. Present your findings in pictorial or diagrammatic format, and add your comments explaining how the examples you have chosen could be played as both unpleasant and comic.

6 A futuristic all-action movie

You are a script writer commissioned by a Hollywood director to write a version of *A Midsummer Night's Dream*. It will be set in the future and modelled on such blockbuster films as *Star Wars* and *Lord of the Rings*. In pairs, work on one short scene and invent some suggestions to present at a script conference which will be held tomorrow.

7 *Get Over It*

Get Over It is a film that uses *A Midsummer Night's Dream* as a backdrop to a high-school love story. Released in 2002, it stars Kirsten Dunst. If you have the opportunity to see it, you will find it's great fun and has imaginative ideas on adapting the play and involving music.

What is the play about?

A Midsummer Night's Dream is a play about love, and it shows clearly that 'the course of true love never did run smooth'. It is a comedy, so traditionally it should end happily, but with problems to solve along the way. At times the play presents threatening and frightening moments for its central characters, with scenes of dramatic tension, hurt and humiliation interspersed with farce and comedy.

The play begins with plans to celebrate a wedding. Theseus, duke of Athens, and Hippolyta, queen of the Amazons, have been at war but now are to marry to ensure future peace. Their planning for a happy future is interrupted by Egeus, with a problem between four young lovers that he demands Theseus should solve. Much of the rest of the play focuses on the attempts of these lovers to sort out their tangled situation.

The play has three main groups of characters

- The lovers (and Hippolyta and Theseus) are rich, indulged individuals primarily concerned with their love lives and how to get their own way. The lovers are obviously very young, and the action of the play will to some extent allow them to grow up and become more perceptive.
- The Mechanicals are workers from Athens. They are keen to gain respect by performing before the duke and earning the 'sixpence a day' they will be paid if their play is chosen.
- The fairies are less easy to pin down as a group because they can be interpreted in a wide variety of ways. They are often the most memorable group of characters in the play because of the imaginative nature of the characterisation and the richness of their language.

There are also three storylines

- The problematic love story of the young lovers: Hermia, Lysander, Helena and Demetrius.
- The Mechanicals' attempts to rehearse and be chosen to perform their play at Theseus's wedding.
- The conflict between the king and queen of the fairies, Oberon and Titania, and how it is resolved.

These storylines all unite as Shakespeare cleverly contrives to have the characters in the same wood on the same night but for differing purposes. The lovers are never aware of the fairies, who cause greater turmoil in their relationships before order is restored. The Mechanicals have contact with the fairy world, with Bottom used as a victim of Puck's humiliation and Oberon's revenge. The lovers do not see the Mechanicals until the final act, when they watch them perform their version of *Pyramus and Thisbe*, which partly parodies the lovers' own situation.

A Midsummer Night's Dream is a play about **love and relationships**. A closely related theme is the difference between 'doting' and 'love', something like the distinction between fancying someone and loving them. The play also presents love as a kind of **madness**, showing that 'reason and love keep little company together'. The variety of relationships provides parallels and contrasts, allowing a range of other themes to be explored, particularly **conflict** and **change**.

Shakespeare dramatises the conflict in each relationship, and shows what changes result as each conflict is resolved. Egeus attempts to force his will on his daughter, but she shows she is capable of defying him. The unrequited love of Helena for Demetrius is also presented as a conflict, and because of her hurt and bitterness she betrays her best friend. Driven by frustration, Demetrius behaves aggressively towards Helena. Hippolyta and Theseus's relationship begins with the conflict of war, and Oberon and Titania are at odds, causing disruption to the natural world.

By the end of Act 3, the lovers are at each other's throats. Helena and Hermia quarrel in a spiteful, abusive way; and Lysander and Demetrius try to kill each other. The relationships of the lovers are punctuated by moments of confusion ('I am amazed, and know not what to say'), mockery ('they have conjoined all three / To fashion this false sport in spite of me'), and pain ('Can you do me greater harm than hate?').

In the final act Pyramus and Thisbe die for love of each other, but the four lovers and Theseus and Hippolyta are all happily united, and the fairies ensure future harmony:

So shall all the couples three
Ever true in loving be . . .

◆ Discuss and make notes on how all the lovers in the play provide similarities and contrasts, and how they highlight certain themes: Theseus/Hippolyta, Lysander/Hermia, Helena/Demetrius, Titania/Oberon, Titania/Bottom – don't forget Pyramus and Thisbe.

Characters

Rupert Everett as Oberon in the 1999 film.

Oberon

The audience first learns from Puck of Oberon's anger against Titania, and so is prepared for his dominant presence on stage. Thematically there are links between Oberon and the other male characters in the play. For example, both he and Theseus are powerful men who subdue the women they love. The mortal and the fairy worlds are presented as male-dominated societies. Oberon is fascinated by the humans' behaviour and actively involves himself in their relationships. Titania accuses him of amorous interest in a number of mythical women; he interferes in the lovers' complex relationships and attends the blessing of their wedding beds at the end. So it may be love, not power, that is his motivation.

Oberon has impressive magical powers that make him – and Puck – fascinating to watch. The invisibility which enables them to overhear mortal talk can be presented as either amusing or sinister. Oberon's magic and Puck's ability to 'Put a girdle round about the earth' allows for the use of trapdoors, lighting effects, hidden wires, and mirrors. The 'love-in-idleness' flower can be perceived as the absolute abuse of power as it interferes with emotions, or as the ultimate righter of wrongs. Certainly Oberon's focus at the end is on marriage and the family.

Titania

Titania is presented as a regal figure, sure of her power and importance. During her struggle with Oberon she defies him and refuses to submit to his bullying. She certainly dominates their first encounter, leaving him spluttering threats after her: 'Thou shalt not from this grove / Till I torment thee for this injury.'

After her initial assertive behaviour, Oberon does indeed succeed in tormenting her. Her relationship with Oberon is obviously sexual, with constant accusations of jealousy and betrayal. Her punishment for non-compliance is to fall in love with the translated Bottom: 'What angel wakes me from my flowery bed?' This relationship is amusing because of the irony of a beautiful fairy queen believing herself in love with an arrogant, ugly man who looks like an ass. Whilst retaining her authoritative nature – 'Out of this wood do not desire to go: / Thou shalt remain here, whether thou wilt or no' – she is truly enraptured with her hairy-faced love. Even Oberon begins to pity her. When she awakes, she immediately recalls her 'dream' and her return to her 'real' world is accompanied by music and dancing.

It is important to think through what Shakespeare intends as his primary purpose with this significant character. She has strong links with the natural world, as her 'forgeries of jealousy' speech (Act 2 Scene 1, lines 81–117) makes clear, and her language is full of natural and cosmic imagery. She is also a mother figure and wants to protect the 'little changeling boy'. By the end of the play she is reunited with Oberon and her role, with him, appears to be to bless the marriages of the newly wed mortals. However, in order to regain her own marital bliss she has had to suffer a cruel indignity and give in to Oberon's wishes.

Puck

Puck keeps Oberon amused with his antics: 'I jest to Oberon, and make him smile . . .'. He is an enigmatic character, difficult to read and capable of being presented on the stage in a variety of ways. He has been played by adult men and women actors as well as by children. As a character he certainly is a lot of fun; he indulges in great merriment at the expense of the humans with whom he comes into contact. In the early description of his knavery he sounds immature in the pleasure he gains from people's indignities and misfortunes.

Sometime for threefoot stool mistaketh me;
Then slip I from her bum, down topples she . . .

Puck is Oberon's servant. His master seems to have affection for him: 'My gentle Puck' and 'Welcome, wanderer.' Oberon is well aware of the true nature of his messenger's 'mad spirit' and will happily blame him when things go wrong:

This is thy negligence. Still thou mistak'st,
Or else committ'st thy knaveries wilfully.

Shakespeare appears to enjoy Puck, and uses him as a running commentary on the absurdities of the mortals. An audience can feel that Puck is right when he exclaims 'Lord, what fools these mortals be!'

How much Puck deliberately undermines the humans for his own pleasure and how much he makes the most of their mistakes is open to interpretation:

And those things do best please me
That befall prepost'rously.

But at the end of the play, almost admitting that all the trickery was intentional, he asks the audience not to be 'offended' as all 'is mended'. It is interesting that in a play about power and control Shakespeare gives the final lines to the servant and not the master.

Puck in Glyndebourne Festival Opera's *A Midsummer Night's Dream* 2001

Bottom

For many people, Bottom is the most memorable character in the play because he is the funniest, he is magically transformed into an ass, and the queen of the fairies falls in love with him. The humour is partly generated by the situation Bottom finds himself in, partly by his lack of self-awareness and partly because we all recognise him and his faults. Bottom is very human.

Bottom is pompous. In the 1999 film (see p. 156) he was presented as a character who feels superior to his colleagues. He is, however, fully involved in their play and its rehearsals and, although Quince is the director, Bottom has a tendency to take over: 'let me play Thisbe too. I'll speak in a monstrous little voice'. His self-belief, which is so misplaced, is also infectious and highlights his enthusiasm. His work-mates do not appear to resent him, and call him 'sweet bully Bottom!' They are distraught when he goes missing and cannot conceive of how they could perform their play without him: 'he hath simply the best wit of any handicraft man in Athens'.

Kevin Kline as Bottom in the 1999 film of the play.

With the most wonderful irony, Puck places an ass's head on Bottom, making it clear what he thinks of this character. Bottom is the only mortal to have a relationship with a fairy, and this relationship is intriguing. Both Titania and Bottom are the victims of cruel magical tricks and their brief 'love' affair is the result. When he wakes from his dream, the audience wonders if he has become a wiser man: 'I have had a dream, / past the wit of man to say what dream it was.' Shakespeare makes Bottom's performance as Pyramus as amateurish and as funny as the audience could wish, and some people's final impression is that he is still an ass.

Other characters

Hermia is a young woman with many problems. She lives at a time when a father had absolute authority over his daughter's choice of husband. Unfortunately, Hermia is in love with Lysander and her father is insisting that she marry Demetrius. Although she lacks real power, it is clear from the beginning that Hermia is confident and willing to assert her views, taking centre stage to explain them: 'I would my father looked but with my eyes.' She is also willing to defy and humiliate her father publicly by agreeing to run away with Lysander. This is similar to another of Shakespeare's leading female characters, Desdemona, who defies her father to marry the man of her choice, Othello.

Lysander, Hermia, Demetrius and Helena in the wood.

Hermia and Helena have had a very close relationship from childhood and the situation obviously puts strain on that friendship. Hermia may well feel smug about Helena's lack of success in love: 'The more I hate, the more he follows me.' Both Hermia and Helena are loyal to the men they love and they end up happily paired with the men of their choice. It is clear to see that through the lovers Shakespeare is exploring male fickleness, but the two girls are not without their faults. Hermia is presented as assertive to the point of aggression. Helena says of her:

O, when she is angry she is keen and shrewd;
She was a vixen when she went to school . . .

Hermia is able to defend herself and is the dominant female of the pair. Helena is wary of her and it may well be this strength of character that both men find so attractive.

Helena starts the play at a low point in her life. She is very much in love with Demetrius, a young man who once courted her. He now wants to marry Hermia and has consequently rejected Helena. This has not altered her feelings, and she cannot understand his change of heart. She is conscious that there is something about Hermia that has attracted him:

O, teach me how you look, and with what art
You sway the motion of Demetrius' heart.

Although she makes much of the notion of sisterhood, 'Both warbling of one song, both in one key,' Helena is the only female in the play who is guilty of real disloyalty with her disclosure to Demetrius of the elopement plan. Her pursuit of Demetrius when he is chasing another woman is undignified:

I am your spaniel; and, Demetrius,
The more you beat me I will fawn on you.

An audience will sympathise with Helena as the victim of unrequited love, but might be in two minds about the way she copes with it. It is interesting that, although she achieves her happiness with Demetrius at the end, it is only after he is under the influence of Oberon's magic love potion.

Lysander is a very confident man, despite the problems that he and Hermia face at the beginning. Buoyed by the knowledge of a way out of the situation and confident of Hermia's love, he is not undermined by Egeus's lack of support, Demetrius's competition, or Theseus's decision:

You have her father's love, Demetrius;
Let me have Hermia's – do you marry him.

Shakespeare presents Lysander as a proactive lover. He plans the elopement, but then loses his way in the wood. In some ways he is a stereotype; he tries hard to persuade Hermia to sleep with him and when confronted with Demetrius's opposition he resorts to fighting.

Demetrius appears much less likeable than Lysander. He seems to be a major cause of the love problem. Why Egeus prefers him we never know. He does not say much in the first scene, but what he does say appears arrogant: 'Lysander, yield / Thy crazèd title to my certain right.' He seems rather careless of Hermia's lack of interest. Even less favourable is his rejection of Helena and his indifference to the hurt he has caused her. His behaviour to Helena in the woods is abusive and aggressive.

Theseus and **Hippolyta** are the first two characters on the stage. Through them we are introduced immediately to the play's main themes of marriage:

Now, fair Hippolyta, our nuptial hour
Draws on apace . . .

and conflict:

Hippolyta, I wooed thee with my sword . . .

Both characters and their story of war and wooing are based on Greek myth. In a play which presents three contrasting worlds, the mythological basis for Theseus and Hippolyta appears to make them closely parallel the fairies. However, they never come into contact with the fairy world. They seem more closely connected to the lovers and the fairies through the exploration of sexual relationships than through linked mythical origins.

Theseus has been played in many ways on stage: as an autocratic politician, a lecherous rogue, a battle-weary young man, and an elderly general. What his personality is like, each audience or reader must decide. Whether his talk of love to Hippolyta is merely politic affectation, 'four happy days bring in / Another moon' – or genuine feeling – 'but O, methinks, how slow / This old moon wanes!', is open to interpretation.

Theseus is very much in charge in Act 1 Scene 1. It is problematic for an audience to make a judgement about a man who describes his own marriage and Hermia's death in the same short speech. Here he wholly supports Egeus's demands, and yet the next day he says 'Egeus, I will overbear your will'. Shakespeare does not make it clear what has caused this about-face; perhaps Theseus is a romantic at heart and finds himself moved by young love. Some productions show Hippolyta encouraging him towards this more feeling response. In Act 5 Theseus presents as a ruler sensitive to his workers by choosing the Mechanicals' play:

For never anything can be amiss
When simpleness and duty tender it.

Hippolyta only speaks twenty-eight lines in the play and may seem passive: she does not involve herself at all in the lovers' plight in Act 1, leaving all the decision making to Theseus. But Shakespeare presents her as a confident and thoughtful woman:

I love not to see wretchedness o'ercharged,
And duty in his service perishing.

The language of *A Midsummer Night's Dream*

Old language

Shakespeare's language may seem complex and difficult when you first encounter it. With time, this impression fades. It becomes easier, but Shakespeare's language remains a challenge.

◆ Working in pairs, divide the words explained on six left-hand pages into those that are easy to understand, perhaps with a little help, and those which seem to have no link with modern English.

One thing to consider is that, of all the major writers in English, Shakespeare uses the largest number of different words, more than four times as many as most authors. He also uses many different meanings of words – he obviously enjoyed playing with language.

Shakespeare can also be hard to understand because today's world is so different from that of four hundred years ago. Some speeches clearly display that difference, as in Act 2 Scene 1, lines 35–8:

That frights the maidens of the villagery,
Skim milk, and sometimes labour in the quern,
And bootless make the breathless housewife churn,
And sometime make the drink to bear no barm . . .

Here, the agricultural England of the 1590s, when the play was probably written, is much in evidence. But even given that the play is set in legendary Athens, not in Shakespeare's England, there is very little that refers directly to Shakespeare's day only.

◆ Make a list of some other examples in the play where the language seems to refer closely to the world of the 1590s and could not really apply to our own day.

Literary language

Shakespeare's language isn't just old, it's literary. For *A Midsummer Night's Dream*, Shakespeare drew upon many other kinds of writing and stories: Greek and Roman mythology, folk tales and legends, and old plays. His language is also shaped for the Elizabethan stage. Unlike some of today's writers for film and television, Elizabethan playwrights often used complex and playful language, rather than trying to be realistic.

This is one of the reasons why Shakespeare's language is not the same as the ordinary speech we use in daily life. The idea that people in Shakespeare's day spoke as the characters in his plays is not correct; they certainly did not speak in rhyme! Why did Shakespeare not use the ordinary speech of real people? In writing much of the play in verse, he was following the stage conventions of the time. Listen carefully to what people around you really say, at home or at school. Would you like to see a play that accurately copied genuine conversations?

There are times when the language in speeches seems to run away with itself, as in Bottom's lines 205–7 in Act 4 Scene 1, where Shakespeare uses the Bible as his guide (see p. 113):

> The eye of man hath not heard, the ear of man hath not seen, /
> man's hand is not able to taste, his tongue to conceive, nor his heart /
> to report what my dream was!

Shakespeare also uses **alliteration** to highlight the comedy implicit in the literary limitations of the Mechanicals:

> Whereat with blade, with bloody, blameful blade,
>   He bravely broached his boiling bloody breast . . .

◆ Watch a TV drama and think about which aspects of the dialogue mimic real speech; which have a distinct purpose, to move the story on or to narrate something about a character's past; and which characters speak in a way that you never really hear in a conversation.

Imagery

Shakespeare seems to have thought in images and *A Midsummer Night's Dream* abounds in imagery (sometimes called 'figures' or 'figurative language'). Imagery is created by vivid words and phrases that conjure up emotionally charged mental pictures or associations in the imagination. Imagery provides insight into character, and gives pleasure as it stirs the audience's imagination. It deepens the dramatic impact of particular moments or moods.

Imagery works well as a way to describe love. Lysander shows his love and concern when he says to Hermia:

> How now, my love? Why is your cheek so pale?
> How chance the roses there do fade so fast?

Helena, because of her unhappy situation, describes love as 'Cupid painted blind'. And at the end of the play Demetrius describes his renewed love for Helena with an image which links love and health:

> But like a sickness did I loathe this food.
> But, as in health come to my natural taste . . .

Problems in love and conflict are also described in terms of storms and bad weather. Hermia describes her tears as a 'tempest of my eyes', and Titania's 'forgeries of jealousy' speech (Act 2 Scene 1, lines 81–117) is filled with extreme images – 'contagious fogs', 'whistling wind' – which create a clear picture of a world in torment because of her 'wrath' with Oberon.

There is a predominance of natural imagery in the play. This is to some extent due to Shakespeare's presentation of the fairies. The natural imagery also creates pictures of the link between the wood and the situations the characters find themselves in. There was little scenery when the play was performed in Shakespeare's time; the playwright's language conveyed a clear impression of the setting to the audience. When Puck torments the Mechanicals (Act 3 Scene 1, lines 89–93), he uses an abundance of frightening imagery so that the audience can picture the scene:

> Through bog, through bush, through brake, through briar;
> Sometime a horse I'll be, sometime a hound,
>   A hog, a headless bear, sometime a fire,
> And neigh, and bark, and grunt, and roar, and burn,
> Like horse, hound, hog, bear, fire at every turn.

A few lines later (103–5) Bottom responds with his own more comforting natural imagery to show he is not afraid:

> The ousel cock so black of hue,
>   With orange-tawny bill,
> The throstle with his note so true,
>   The wren with little quill –

Shakespeare uses the moon as a recurring image in the play for a variety of effects. Theseus's image 'Chanting faint hymns to the cold fruitless moon' describes Hermia's life if she chooses to become a nun. Earlier, he used the moon as a marker for the slow passing of time until his wedding day: 'how slow / This old moon wanes!' And in Act 1 Scene 1, lines 9–11, Hippolyta links the moon with night-time and dreams:

And then the moon, like to a silver bow
New bent in heaven, shall behold the night
Of our solemnities.

Most of the play takes place at night, and Shakespeare was keen that his language conjured up the tone and atmosphere of a night in the wood: a place of no light except moonlight, in which his characters stumbled around, feeling more vulnerable than they did in Athens. This is the world of another group of characters who are definitely at home in their surroundings and have the upper hand. It is an excellent place to explore the vagaries of mortal love and the foibles of human beings. The moon becomes a symbol of inconstancy and infidelity, highly relevant to a plotline which explores Lysander and Demetrius's fickleness. Lysander plans to meet Hermia under the light of the 'silver visage' of Phoebe (goddess of the moon, associated with chastity), but when in the wood standing on the grass decked 'with liquid pearl' he behaves in a less chaste and constant way.

The Mechanicals view the moon less as image or symbol. They want a physical representation of the moon in their play: a lantern. They cannot comprehend how language can create a moon, making it real for an audience.

Fascinating and thought-provoking images are those about dreams and reality. When she wakes up after her night in the wood (Act 4 Scene 1, lines 186–7), Hermia comments on the experience:

Methinks I see these things with parted eye,
When everything seems double.

Bottom is also puzzled by his memory of events and thinks it is 'past the wit of man to say what dream it was. Man is but an ass / if he go about to expound this dream' (Act 4 Scene 1, line 201). Bottom is trying to be philosophical here and to reflect upon the meaning of his vision, but his mixed-up imagery makes it even more confusing, and amusing for the audience. This is exactly what Oberon intended when he declared in Act 3 Scene 2, lines 370–1:

When they next wake, all this derision
Shall seem a dream and fruitless vision . . .

The play is full of images of dreams. It ends with Theseus commenting on the Mechanicals' play: 'The best in this kind are but shadows; and the worst are no / worse, if imagination amend them' (Act 5 Scene 1, lines 205–6). And at lines 403–6 Puck tells the audience to think:

> That you have but slumbered here
> While these visions did appear;
> And this weak and idle theme,
> No more yielding but a dream . . .

Shakespeare's imagery uses metaphor, simile and personification. All are comparisons which substitute one thing (the image) for another (the thing described).

A **simile** compares one thing to another, using 'as' or 'like'. Demetrius describes his love for Hermia, 'Melted as the snow', and Lysander says he will shake Hermia from him 'like a serpent'. Earlier Helena describes her friendship with Hermia as 'like to a double cherry'. Sometimes similes can be used for comic effect. Thisbe, attempting romantic imagery, describes Pyramus: 'His eyes were green as leeks.'

A **metaphor** is also a comparison, suggesting that two dissimilar things are actually the same. To put it another way, a metaphor borrows one word or phrase to express another. Helena uses a humiliating image when she says to Demetrius (Act 2 Scene 1, lines 203–4):

> I am your spaniel; and, Demetrius,
> The more you beat me I will fawn on you.

In Act 3, when the lovers are in a potion-induced confusion over their relationships, they use metaphor to put each other down. Lysander calls Hermia 'loathed medicine! O hated potion', whilst Hermia calls Helena a 'painted maypole'.

Personification turns all kinds of things into persons, giving them human feelings or attributes: 'And to that place the sharp Athenian law / Cannot pursue us.'

Antithesis

LYSANDER   The course of true love never did run smooth;
                    But either it was different in blood –
HERMIA   O cross! too high to be enthralled to low.
LYSANDER   Or else misgraffèd in respect of years –
HERMIA   O spite! too old to be engaged to young.
LYSANDER   Or else it stood upon the choice of friends –
HERMIA   O hell, to choose love by another's eyes!

The first of these lines from Act 1 Scene 1, lines 134–40, is now proverbial. The exclamations which follow ('O cross!' 'O spite!' 'O hell') are absurd and comical, but literary and highly patterned as well (notice the echoing rhythms of the last five lines). Shakespeare is using one of his favourite language devices, **antithesis** – setting words or phrases against each other to heighten the sense of conflict (high/low, old/young). Try to find more examples of antithesis, and one or two other moments like this where the language might seem to overwhelm or contradict the emotions.

Verse and prose

Although it has a good deal of rhyme, more of *A Midsummer Night's Dream* is written in blank verse: unrhymed verse with a five-beat rhythm (iambic pentameter). Each line has five iambs (feet), each with one stressed (/) and one unstressed syllable (×):

$$× \quad / \quad × \quad / \quad × \quad / \quad × \quad / \quad × \quad /$$
This man with lanthorn, dog, and bush of thorn

The court and the fairies mainly use this kind of verse, but (apart from their Pyramus and Thisbe play) the Mechanicals' speeches are in prose. Thus the language of the characters reflects their social position, as well as creating different kinds of comedy.

Shakespeare also uses other metres, most obviously four-stress rhythm as in 'You spotted snakes with double tongue', and in the final sixty-seven lines of the play.

◆ Try writing a modern speech that fits the verse pattern of iambic pentameter (five stresses in each line).

Language and character

The language of the characters – the words, patterns and images they use – creates their characters as much as their actions or the plot.

◆ Examine the speeches of your favourite character in order to identify the patterns of language they use, and to what effect.
◆ Create a presentation that concentrates on the language of the play. Make displays that will put across what you feel are some of the most important features of Shakespeare's language:
  – famous favourite lines from the play;
  – photographs of actors next to the lines from the script;
  – your own attempts at writing like Shakespeare;
  – drawings of Shakespeare's verbal 'pictures' next to his verse;
  – examples of different kinds of wordplay and humour.

A Midsummer Night's Dream in performance

The importance of courtship and marriage to the play led many people to believe that *A Midsummer Night's Dream* was written as an entertainment for an aristocratic wedding, but this is almost certainly not true. It is about love and relationships. It is also about change: growing up and the move from single life to marriage. How productions of the play have been staged over the years since it was written have to some extent been formed by contemporary social attitudes to marriage. A Victorian audience may well have had a very different view from a modern one towards Hermia's refusal to yield to her father's wishes and her decision to elope with Lysander. A production would also respond to a contemporary audience's perception of the whole notion of fairies, magic and the supernatural.

A Midsummer Night's Dream has been the subject of numerous paintings over the years, including this of Titania and Bottom, painted in 1848 by Sir Edward Landseer. The fairies in the play captured the imagination of the art world throughout the eighteenth and nineteenth centuries.

Music and dance have always played a large part in productions of the play. Directors often commission composers to write original scores for new productions. It has inspired the writing of both a ballet and operas. Operatic versions of Shakespeare's plays cut the language very heavily or rewrite it. All the action and characterisation in a ballet are interpreted through music and dance. Below is a picture of Oberon and Puck from a Sadler's Wells Ballet production in 1983.

When *A Midsummer Night's Dream* was first performed on stage, all the female parts were played by young boys. This issue is amusingly explored through the character of Francis Flute and his response to being cast as Thisbe, 'Nay, faith, let me not play a woman: I have a beard coming.'

There were few props and little in the way of sets. The audience had to imagine the contrast between the first scene in Duke Theseus's palace and the night scenes in the wood. In this they were greatly helped by Shakespeare's imagery and the actors' responses. The actors wore expensive costumes in keeping with the fashions and style of the time.

Modern productions sometimes use detailed and opulent sets and costumes, as in the picture above. It shows Act 1 Scene 1 and sets the play in the later part of the Victorian era.

Peter Brook's production of the play in 1970 (see p. 169) presented a radical new interpretation. The stage was spartan and stark, the costumes were simple and in primary colours. The fairies were shown suspended above the stage on trapeze-like swings and were lowered up and down for their interactions with the mortals. It has proved to be a very influential production and many companies, directors and costume and set designers have imitated and developed these ideas.

Oberon and Puck enter the stage from above in Peter Brook's 1970 production of the play.

Titania and her fairies have been presented in very different ways. The photograph on page 170 (top) is of a 1989 Royal Shakespeare Company production. It shows Titania with pixie ears and wings. Her fairies are children who look decidedly naughty in their ballet tutus and clumpy boots. The production at the Globe Theatre in London in 2002 (p. 170, bottom) shows a very different Titania. Here, confronting Oberon, she wears a nightdress. Her adult male fairies wear pyjamas.

◆ Compile a list of the dramatic gains and losses in presenting the fairies in these two different ways. Which do you prefer? Why?

A 2001 production had an all-female cast playing the Mechanicals. Bottom was played by Dawn French (who appears on the front cover as Bottom transformed). This is gender role reversal, but not in the way that Shakespeare's own audience experienced it. Talk together, then write notes on the considerations you think influenced this casting decision and the effects it had on characterisation and the development of relationships.

'Let me play the lion too. I will roar . . .'

When studying or acting in a Shakespeare play, one question always arises: 'What does it all mean?' The answer is that it means different things at different times and also many things at once. *A Midsummer Night's Dream* has been acted for over four hundred years and people are still debating and exploring its different meanings and interpretations. The complexity of the play and its language is part of the appeal of Shakespeare. It is an exploration in which there is no final, complete and 'right' explanation. Perhaps Bottom was right (Act 4 Scene 1, lines 200–1:

I have had a most rare vision. I have had a dream, / past the wit of man to say what dream it was.

William Shakespeare
1564–1616

1564 Born Stratford-upon-Avon, eldest son of John and Mary Shakespeare.

1582 Marries Anne Hathaway of Shottery, near Stratford.

1583 Daughter, Susanna, born.

1585 Twins, son and daughter, Hamnet and Judith, born.

1592 First mention of Shakespeare in London. Robert Greene, another playwright, described Shakespeare as 'an upstart crow beautified with our feathers . . .'. Greene seems to have been jealous of Shakespeare. He mocked Shakespeare's name, calling him 'the only Shake-scene in a country' (presumably because Shakespeare was writing successful plays).

1595 A shareholder in The Lord Chamberlain's Men, an acting company that became extremely popular.

1596 Son Hamnet dies, aged 11.
Father, John, granted arms (acknowledged as a gentleman).

1597 Buys New Place, the grandest house in Stratford.

1598 Acts in Ben Jonson's *Every Man in His Humour*.

1599 Globe Theatre opens on Bankside. Performances in the open air.

1601 Father, John, dies.

1603 James I grants Shakespeare's company a royal patent: The Lord Chamberlain's Men become The King's Men and play about twelve performances each year at court.

1607 Daughter, Susanna, marries Dr John Hall.

1608 Mother, Mary, dies.

1609 The King's Men begin performing indoors at Blackfriars Theatre.

1610 Probably returns from London to live in Stratford.

1616 Daughter, Judith, marries Thomas Quiney.
Dies. Buried in Holy Trinity Church, Stratford-upon-Avon.

The plays and poems
(no one knows exactly when he wrote each play)

1589–95 *The Two Gentlemen of Verona, The Taming of the Shrew, First, Second and Third Parts of King Henry VI, Titus Andronicus, King Richard III, The Comedy of Errors, Love's Labour's Lost, A Midsummer Night's Dream, Romeo and Juliet, King Richard II* (and the long poems *Venus and Adonis* and *The Rape of Lucrece*).

1596–9 *King John, The Merchant of Venice, First and Second Parts of King Henry IV, The Merry Wives of Windsor, Much Ado About Nothing, King Henry V, Julius Caesar* (and probably the *Sonnets*).

1600–5 *As You Like It, Hamlet, Twelfth Night, Troilus and Cressida, Measure for Measure, Othello, All's Well That Ends Well, Timon of Athens, King Lear.*

1606–11 *Macbeth, Antony and Cleopatra, Pericles, Coriolanus, The Winter's Tale, Cymbeline, The Tempest.*

1613 *King Henry VIII, The Two Noble Kinsmen* (both probably with John Fletcher).

1623 Shakespeare's plays published as a collection (now called the First Folio).